11

COLLE

Also by Bill Manhire

Poetry

Malady
The Elaboration
The Old Man's Example
How to Take Off Your Clothes at the Picnic
Good Looks
Zoetropes
Milky Way Bar
My Sunshine
Sheet Music: Poems 1967–1982
What to Call Your Child

Fiction

The Brain of Katherine Mansfield
The New Land
South Pacific

Non-fiction

Maurice Gee
Doubtful Sounds: Essays and Interviews

As Editor

New Zealand Listener Stories
Some Other Country
Six by Six
Soho Square
100 New Zealand Poems
Mutes & Earthquakes
Spectacular Babies

BILL MANHIRE

Collected Poems

CARCANET

First published in New Zealand
in 2001 by
Victoria University Press

First published in Great Britain
in 2001 by
Carcanet Press Limited
4th Floor, Conavon Court
12–16 Blackfriars Street
Manchester M3 5BQ

A CIP catalogue record for this book
is available from the British Library

ISBN 1 85754 537 0

The publisher acknowledges financial assistance
from the Arts Council of England.

Set in Monotype Bembo by XL Publishing Services, Tiverton
Printed and bound in England by SRP Ltd, Exeter

CONTENTS

THE ELABORATION

THE OLD MAN'S EXAMPLE

HOW TO TAKE OFF YOUR CLOTHES
AT THE PICNIC

GOOD LOOKS

ZOETROPES

MILKY WAY BAR

MY SUNSHINE

WHAT TO CALL YOUR CHILD

ANTARCTIC FIELD NOTES

FOR MARION

THE ELABORATION

LOVE POEM

There is no question
of choice, but it takes
a long time

Love's vacancies, the eye
& cavity, track
back to embraces

where the spine bends
& quietens
like smoke in the earth.

Your tongue, touching on song,
darkens all songs. Your touch
is almost a signature.

A HOPE FOR FRANK AND ANNE

It is the pitchy night. She has
The palest neck. She munches
Chocolates, she stares at flowers.

Outside tall Frank a-courting
Bends above his cane. He taps
Upon the window, raising

His hat to the stars: and ancient worms
Twist in the hearth, they set off
Up the chimney, climbing to the moon.

While in its deep cave the earth
Cramps. But the lady's hand retains
The cry of rain, the lady's breast

Awakens revel. Small birds gather
Together in dark places. They cry
Out of an old season.

THE OCCUPATION, AGAINST TIME

Somewhere all the wrong reasons
Vanish, as they care to,
Among the remains of lips

And somewhere, at a great distance,
My hand opens, to display
My hand: her breath is

A soft paw touching me out
Of its own darkness, where I see
The barks of trees and her eyes

Shining from a hidden place,
As my bones grow away from me,
Her body being a close thing.

POEM

When we touch,
forests enter our bodies.

The dark wind shakes the branch.
The dark branch shakes the wind.

THE PROOF

She did not speak to me yesterday
All day there was silence
By this I was hurt
I walked down the street
Unable to think of anything
But her: that is how these things
Affect you
        today she says
Good morning, kisses me
So I am sullen, I do not reply
I think I must love her

THE ELABORATION

There was a way out of here:
it went off in the night
licking its lips.

The door flaps like a great wing:
I make fists at the air
and long to weaken.

Ah, to visit you
is the plain thing,
and I shall not come to it.

WATCHING ALISON IN WINTER

She is even gone now
Out of the high doorway

Her hand being a window
A chapel of fingers

Oh blue darknesses, pale stones
Deep stars of the river

My voice is only a voice
It cannot name this space

The thump of a dead heart
The dust of a wrist

Here, madam, are your oceans
She is even gone now

YOUR ABSENCE

Your absence is a hurt
I would bring to no one:
It is a place
For entertaining friends and waiting.
I shall always ask you in.

THE WHITE PEBBLE

1
For three years
it slept by me
tied at my love's wrist
white smoke in the pillow

2
I use the white pebble
to hold a book open
at the page I want

& write words
in the light
it casts
when the moon rises

3
If you pick it up
it plunges away
the weight plunges

4
Sometimes I throw it
in a woman's lap
& cast her asleep

or give it to friends
commencing a marriage

5
Here it is
falling through
the air

★

a small regret

a feather

6
If you happen on
the white pebble
it is the colour of a stream

(a man is sitting close by
eating sandwiches)

TWO SONGS FOR MORAG

1

In the month of wind the bones
Of cattle turning over
In the wind

And you kneeling among sand
Pardoning the fishes

Morag Morag

Who will tend your ridiculous garden?
How will the crops fatten?

2

I touch you with rocks about you
Your shape gathered
In weakness

Availing itself of darkness

Ah Morag, my
Patience, my lively
Place, it is

Not my doing: the
Spider building in
The cave of

Bone, trees
Bending and trees
Bending

THE SPELL

Each time I sneeze
the devil steps by me.
He pours the hours
into my wrists, minute
by minute.

That dream; in which I inhabit
my father's shoulder, a stale
whisky smell.

My friends send over their
daughters for safe-keeping. Such
commonplace girls,
all in aprons.

They smile
nevertheless, they manage it.
One is a bird, one a broken stone.

IN THE TENT, ELCHE

Since I need something else,
a machine with gold stars
in it, an ocean tossing with
fish, I hold you in my arms.

The rain was stopping just
as we began to talk about it.
How we complain to enter the earth,
like water falling from its cages.

THE PRAYER

I
What do you take
away with you?

Here is the rain,
a second-hand miracle,
collapsing out of Heaven.

It is the language of
earth, lacking an audience,
but blessing the air.

What light it brings
with it, how far
it is.

★

I stayed a minute
& the garden
was full of voices.

2
I am tired again
while you are crossing

the river, on a bridge
six inches under water.

Small trees grow out of
the planks & shade the water.

Likewise, you are full of
good intentions
& shade the trees with your body.

3
Lord, Lord
in my favourite religion
You would have to be
a succession of dreams.

In each of them
I'd fall asleep,

scarred like a
rainbow, no doubt,
kissing the visible bone.

THE RIVER

The moon casts our shadows
into the water. They drift over pebbles,
watching us leave them.

THE VOYAGE

I
All night water laps
the hedges. I hold you in the middle
of the air.

2
Don't sleep
all night. It is pitch

black, but since
there is a vista, let

your throat be
the lantern.

3
Since there is
a window, let us

open it.

4
Let us dress
for a voyage. Let me

go out, with
your voice, to call for you.

THE SEASONS / IF
I WILL SING THERE

for Marion

I
Green tree hung over
a gorge
    pebbles, sound

       of rocks
       & water

filling with mist

   breathing / unfolding

II
horizoned: as the mouth
moving over the
body, the bodies moving

through rain
       faced
together, in
resemblance

       lips, whispered
of

III
yawning by me, caught
in yourself, your
own deep

secret, falling

asleep in
autumn   autumn

when the moon draws through

IV
falling to its
knees

and

gathering promises all
winter
        ice, the length of

a body, *presence*, bound
in light

PAVILION

The house was in the mountains,
perched on the moon's wrist.
We sung, we sang.
I have forgot it.

All day you drew ladies dancing on clouds,
one falling into the open mouth of a book.
It was in the mountains
and I prayed for the swan.
I forget it.

The red pavilion, the red pavilion.
A tree climbed back in its leaves.
Love, good morning,
your body was all freckles.

A DEATH IN THE FAMILY

His face is gone golden with the dusk
You would think he burned, he burned

We came without invitation
We did not follow the highways

Trees we went beneath, bending
Then climbed the stone walls

Golden, golden, and he has not spoken
We sent so many missives

Let us go brother, let us go sister
Open the gates, how can we remain?

He will not answer us
His eyes blaze out beyond us

His face is gone golden with the dusk
You would think he burned, he burned

THE OLD MAN'S EXAMPLE

THE GOD WHO WATCHES
OVER ALL PERHAPS

1
Walking down Princes Street
With ice and no one, I understand
That I am going home.

2
At dawn only the sky is busy,
In a day of its own making:
Beyond it, some god perhaps,
The spreader of crusted ice, watches
Over all: while at his side a woman
Turns, in a desire of sleeping.

3
The ice has its own face,
As I have mine. I walk
On the white shape of prayer, and invite
My heels to walk with me.

POETICS

Talking to you, Chinese poetry
Is a total failure: you button
Up your coat all evening.

And under the stars
I say the names of breakfast cereals
Over and over, stealing someone's
Bottle of milk.

The night bends

Back its great wings.
The moon turns like a bone.

If you inherit pain
You inherit the shoulders of God.

If you inherit agony
It is sheer accident.

THE OLD MAN'S EXAMPLE

These drifting leaves, for instance
That tap my shoulder
Come along with us, they say
There are one or two questions
We should like to ask you

THE CLOWN AT THE DEATH
OF HIS WIFE

Now I am feeling grief
I have received these flowers
Triste I am, triste
Heaven gawps
Please believe that one

THE ORETI RIVER
watching the grown ups

I thrust my
toes down

through white
pebbles

into wet
gravel. They

wriggle
about, like

worms. I think
of the

mice, dressed
up in old

newspapers, dancing
in

the cupboard. I
run into

the
water and

pretend
to drown.

MORAG'S VALEDICTION

Farewell ruins, barren
Footprint where I hid for
Months, farewell cold churches,
I do not care. Now I enter
The forest of lovely trees, it
Swallows all weighty things:
And I circle, moving
Secretly.
              For here it begins,
A gleam in the bone, light
From the skull. Solomon
Dreams. I am
In Solomon's dream.

FOR PRESIDENT JOHNSON ON
THE SHORES OF AMERICA

1
This is our dying season:
It is in the throats of trees,
A drumming among dark stones.

2
His hands magnify the bright coast:
They touch
The skull of the dawn.

3
And we still whisper
Of remarkable loves,
A huge ice dancing on our fingers.

SOUNDING THE DARK
for Charles Brasch

To know his place on earth
and after is no part
of man's concern.

Guessing and praising,
self is a leaf,
falls in self's footprint.

★

Words fail, grant nothing.
The unsteady body ceases.
Beyond time, time passes.

Earth-silence, wound
in the body, crouched
in a swan's wing.

Solitary beyond solitude.

Unearthed.

★

Tick of the clock makes
a silence: footstep of stars.

Neither passing nor passer
light dances and is far

too far; and the words spin,
unwinding sweet and bitter,

passing through dark
and dark, curious to do better.

YOUR ROOM

1
Water seeps through
above the rafters.

This swamp appals us.
At night the frogs wash out

their shirts
and settle back, puffing cigars.

Their mouths glow in the dark
like stars. Behind them the moon floats

in a roped container,
leather casting a shadow.

2
These stones
will make us nostalgic

for carpet. Now and then
we catch sight through the smoke

of animals moving slowly,
half in the earth.

And occasionally a head lifts
among the benevolent flowers.

We are never alone here,
but we can never see

enough of each other – constantly
filling the lantern

with hair, with pebbles.

3
In the next room
your mother sinks in her bed.

Mad for years. Each night

she dreams there's a fish
in her lungs

and wakes up screaming,
unable to say your name.

The frogs make tender
choking noises, which pass

for sorrow. They go hopefully
from house to house

with tokens of flowers.

4
If it were colder
we might embrace.

I shiver, anyway, watching
you fall asleep
on the damp mattress.

The moon rocks gently
in its ashes –

a quiet trembling
that almost wakes you.

5
First light.

There is nothing to see but water,
two frogs on a stone

knotting your hair into lines
which they trail in the water.

When I whisper your name
they nod their heads

and tie it for bait,
casting slowly among the flowers.

BUCKETS

A woman commits suicide
Two houses away.
I ring her up to say goodbye.

I light a fire in the coal-bucket.
Evening, stone upon stone.
I am compiling a list of buckets.

WINGS

This lantern was designed
for my fashionable wrist movements

I am going to let loose the pillows
into the afternoon you went missing from

each part of you turned up to me
a feathery light
some planet from the middle ages

THE VISITOR

after Anna Akhmatova

Everything is as it was that time:
Beyond the dining-room window
The confused snow swirls,
And I have not grown any younger.
Yet some man approached me.

'What is it you want?' I asked.
He said, 'To be with you in hell.'
And I laughed aloud. 'Do you sense
Such trouble ahead for us?'

He raised his dry hand,
Softly touching flowers:
'Tell me how a man kisses you,
How you return the kiss.'

His dull eyes gazed steadily
At the ring on my finger:
His was an evil, cheerful face,
It didn't move a muscle.

Oh he delights greatly, I see,
In his heart's deep assurance
That there's nothing he really needs
And nothing I can refuse him.

POEM

In my songs, quality is a tradition.
Falling asleep is a tradition.
How the waterfall sleeps.
How the water sleeps.
How you fall asleep in water.

In my songs, what you want
overcomes you because you do not know
what you want but you can
easily have it. There and there,
there are thousands of illustrations.

In my songs, your mouth
is my mouth and what's mine is yours.
Your mouth is a mouth underwater,
calling, in pain, words I imagine
and find myself singing.

HOW TO TAKE OFF YOUR CLOTHES AT THE PICNIC

THE INCISION

Snow in the brain, under the skin.
Under the covers, bark and a few branches.
Locomotive nature is coming to find us,
waving its amenable flags. Not that
we are not also going out to find
it, but it is hardly necessary:

we always hated to be successful.
This must be a new episode in our lives,
side by side, with a certainty of capture,
while the leaves sink
into our shoulders like language,
words we are rumoured to live in.

And I don't know you, yawn in the heart,
even when you respect my wishes,
turning back into the steps
of nothing I ever wanted:
there, the lake choked with feathers,
there, the deep wings folded over.

THE POETRY READING

The green fields. The green fields.
How beautiful they are.
How beautiful they are.

This next poem is about the green fields
Which are to be found in England.
They contain certain small animals
Which have chosen to make their life there.

The public has constant access to them.
Not to the animals, as you might
Understandably think, but to the green fields
In which they have chosen to make their homes.

ORNAMENTS

Water: you surface by multiplying.
Then the telephone calls start:
one very beautiful backstage actress,
two comparatively straightforward deliveries,
three blind mice.
Condemned or precocious, do you
really look that bad?

And because we are always
at the beach, going into the water,
I come home and stare at your ornaments:
it's dark and disgraceful
but it makes good sense, especially since
we had the new telephone installed,
the one I hear you hang up on.

I am hung up on you
if you will pardon the expression.
You submerge me like belief, like
tidal waves, and even the home is under.
'I hardly ever see you these days.
We never talk.' My excuse,
your excuse; late afternoon, the plans.

THE COLLECTION

I

All day at the lake we watched
cars, the red guts of mountains.
You lay back at the edge of
water & demonstrated my lack
of perfection: the trick of
the bird, sliding down a rainbow.

Later you bring on all your
effects: & in the garden we discover
the skating-rink, women ticking
with white frost, as if they
mean to go off. A farmer from
Balclutha sends a platoon of sheep

out on to the ice. In their little
boots they are quite graceful.
They surround three women &
shepherd them in for inspection.
You sail out from me, shaking
ice from your shoulders.

2

The room goes back about
one month's journeying,
past a pet cat & a few musicians,
to where a number of people
are celebrating Christmas.

My father is dreaming of
a white mistress. That is
his joke, he is utterly
deluded, but you fit the bill.

My mother is looking for
the arrival of Christ. She needs
only a small opportunity,
only no one will provide it.

In the garden, flowers
thicken with each kiss.
My friends, never in danger,
make a perfect descent from
the tree. The moon drives
light into your spine.

We are all here, with
a smattering of language.
It seems we have gone
overboard for sincerity.

3
Well,

you have become my favourite
neighbour, merely by being
in the right place at the
right time. In mid-flight
on the swing in your garden,
clutching a bucket of clothes-
pegs, hovering over the carrots,
you are my very best friend.

Your journeys are crowded with
little forks: some are mine,
& a few you have on approval.
On New Year's Eve we take up
the collection. You retreat
into the hedge & reach out

your fingers, as if you mean
something by it. Like

the magician's magic hand
depositing the ace of spades
in a lady's knickers.
The music. The music of water.

WINTROUS

Moths have chased you out
Into the snow where
It is all moths. You can hardly
Imagine the neat variety
Of white moths dancing.

In this fashion snow will find
Its way to a small woman: in
A specified season or when
She holds it necessary.

All night her voice overturns
And stands naked, clutching
Itself for warmth. The body is then
Nearly defunct, and stinks of sleep.
The breath is a wound tearing open.

Hence we have invited friends
To an Evening: termed
The Demolishing of Cages.
The wedding of canaries will be witnessed
By candlelight.

Canary marriages are dangerous
To celebrate, and always uncertain.
Consequently their tongues, also,
Are uncertain, while their shadows
Are rarely able to steal over you.

TURTLE

You go by coral and by sands
Looking for cupboards to vanish in.
We sat at the table, all of us.

You ran round the house
In ten seconds flat
Then went the same journey on your hands:
Going away from me bit by bit.

And so I love you bit by bit
Butterfly, you're one of the family.
When you brought the cat in,
Covered with bruises, I laughed

And laughed and laughed. Jack
And Mary and the little rascals
Burn. I slept in an old shirt
And saw you out the window.

So the sheets had dirty fingers.
This is an apology.

THE CONTRACT

Sometimes you are distinctly
childlike. I half expect you
to bring me gifts, some
ordinary purchase out of
nature – a flower,
or a dead sparrow.

And sometimes
you resemble a room
filled with pianos, lacking
all taste.

When you tire of lying out
under the moon, the sea is all
grape & I am in bed
with my portable woman,
tearing along the dotted line.
Then you are most like
the lady in the comic-book, lifted
miles into the air
with your eyes showing it.

I have a method specially
reserved for dealing with you.
It involves a giant wasp
with orange stripes, opening
its wings just before dawn.
Come in, if you get really
sick of it. Let us bury this comfort.

LAST SONNET

There is this photograph of you dancing
which keeps on arriving in the post.
Every morning I send out the dogs,
but they come back whimpering, broken-
boned: i.e.

the mails always get through.
Anne is laughing.
She turned into a tree.
Jane went to Europe,
a death to rocks and flowers.
Carol has had all her hair cut off.

What do you want, waving and
waving, your hands flung
right out of the picture?

THE CALENDAR

In Autumn, the trees give themselves
back into the earth – day after day
and then it is months,
falling asleep with a great satisfaction.
Birds leave off
with their one and only.

There is a sky in the body
we are flying into.
There is a wind pushing clouds about,
lifting our hands to wave back sadly.

We are waving at history, then,
we are waving

at what makes sense to happen.
We still expect sunlight, falling
in a room, a bed with flowers
upon it. I visited you there,
years ago, attending to the days
that passed you by.

SUMMER

1
It is so white.

It divides under the snow.
It wakes alone, a sensational pleasure.

2
Supposing this page is a paddock
under snow, or rather supposing
this page is snow

blanketing the paddock
then these lines

must be tracks in the whiteness
left by animals late at night.

Or fences, or trees
just risking the surface.

3
Possibly the bodies of lovers are also present,
though almost invisible to the naked eye.

4
See?

And occasionally, one supposes,
some marriage may be celebrated.

5
Or, this word may be a boulder,
or this, or this

or this, which is a stone,
on which the poet sits, somewhat alone,
saying, 'Hell, another masterpiece.'

IT IS NEARLY SUMMER

A rubber duck is paddling up the sky.
The world is a constant amazement,
always on the move.
It is nearly summer. It is nearly autumn.

CITY LIFE

Rainy days inside
We starved and fell in love
Small bird
Let's sit here on the roof
And make some decisions about the city

The sandpit's big enough to sleep in
Days and days
With nothing to talk about
Till we both slipped out of the house together
I still can't believe it

Wings and stalks, see how they fly
Our life together under some stairs
Some moonlight entering
Large flowers that last in a jar
Well where will we go from there?

Damp afternoons, the darkness in the garden
Remember I followed you home by night
So tired and turning over
And going at last to sleep then
Not loving you less, but better

THE KISS

The damp sky is eating your hair.
The day drags its branches over.
There is no beautiful rest in which
you can do no wrong. Give me the teeth,

says the universe. You are neither here
nor there, but walking.

The direction you are taking
cries a low welcome
and darkness sinks its bone
in your shoulder. Under the stars
you are fed somewhat on stars.
Their popular wounds light your body.

A tale of grasslands under the sky.
A tale of hesitation.
The tale of a woman, pressing
her breasts against the window.
A tale of hesitation.
A tale of grasslands under the sky.

THE COLLABORATION

For better or worse, you are glad
to be here. The only risk you take
is that we are all in it together.
Your sleeves fill with wind.

Then a woman you want badly
is passing by. Naturally
you are past caring, but nothing
is too much trouble: your hand

is at her waist before you
know it. Soon she is accepting
a ride in your attractive chariot,
the pursuit through the world

which ends in total victory.
You cannot fail to enjoy
yourself because you have
the right approach. You cannot

fail to be happy because we
require it. If you are in love, then
music takes its rightful place
in our hearts. If you are

dying, that is a distinct
improvement. If the clocks
stop forever, you are
always here on the dot.

LEAVING HOME

Poor boy, poor boy

out on the prowl, you pick up your
future wife: she leaves in the morning.
Her lipstick on the mirror reads
'Goodbye' and 'Forever'.

There are small things which live
on your skin and which you take
for granted: the dust of a fever, for instance,
in which you decide to take it easy.

There is the doctor, like the tree
in which you will rest, his head
bending and nodding in the wind
which shakes you. You long for the comfort

of poverty, a photograph into which
you can carry your bruises.
A faint mist shines to make the journey
dangerous, and for better or worse

you make it. You dance on the table
poor boy, you remove your tie,
you adopt a specially relaxed
tone of voice. You applaud your own

good sense.

THE L & R SONG

He shaves off his beard
and he has almost done it.
Nothing is going to have its way now
except him, and he does not want it.
He wants to be nothing.

One supposes, she gave him everything,
life, love,
and the strength to be happy.
Out *there*, he is crippled by laughter.
No one is likely to stop him

except her, and she does not want to.
No one is laughing, likely
to be free, nobody is merely
a body, to be given up easily, lightly,
with nothing on, nowhere to go.

Yet this is the house they are both leaving,
where she sews garments. She has stitched
confidence into the shoulders,
leather into the elbows, until
he is all strength, and leaves her his weakness;

so that she leaves him,
and they both go, underfoot, under duress,
into prediction:
one sings to the other,
they make love,

they fall apart, the children grow.
The song, without words, sung
under nothing: how they leave each other
to it – a note for friends, a ready smile –
how they need to leave it at that.

THE SNOW

Men are singing by the willows
as your boat passes upstream,
drawn by other men, waist-
deep in water. You pass as clearly
over: hands of
the wind, the solemn parting.

In the dream, you fell into
the story, a light
in the mountains, and the people
seeking it. High up, snow
kept falling: its small wings rose
to shake the darkness.

Movement in and out of sleep,
you tell the simple pattern.
Each minute it will soon be evening:
a scarf of earth,
your wrist in earth,
the old sad planet's voices.

ON ORIGINALITY

Poets, I want to follow them all,
out of the forest into the city
or out of the city into the forest.

The first one I throttle.
I remove his dagger
and tape it to my ankle in a shop doorway.
Then I step into the street
picking my nails.

I have a drink with a man
who loves young women.
Each line is a fresh corpse.

There is a girl with whom we make friends.
As he bends over her body
to remove the clothing
I slip the blade between his ribs.

Humming a melody, I take his gun.
I knot his scarf carelessly at my neck, and

I trail the next one into the country.
On the bank of a river I drill
a clean hole in his forehead.

Moved by poetry
I put his wallet in a plain envelope
and mail it to the widow.

I pocket his gun.
This is progress.
For instance, it is nearly dawn.

Now I slide a gun into the gun
and go out looking.

It is a difficult world.
Each word is another bruise.

This is my nest of weapons.
This is my lyrical foliage.

THE IMPORTANCE OF PERSONAL RELATIONSHIPS

Let's just reject
discussion, the safety of
numbers

and go to
sleep in a
serious fashion. Dancing

on God's
veiny wrist, for instance, leaping
the veins: I mean, we

could manage that more
often. *How do*
you do how

do you
do? I am fine thank
you.

THE PROPOSITION

the week it
snowed, the day the
footpaths didn't matter,
I wanted to get

a number of things
straight, but didn't:
and the next day, when
people were out

again, driving, you said
let's take ourselves
off, into the country,
to a cave, or that

kind of expedition: I bent,
tentative, over the
table, and cracked my
knuckles: would you

care to be more
precise about whatever
it is you are
saying, I said

THE PROCEDURE

I spend a lot of time on
the lavatory because my
food is determined never
to leave me. I also play

a lot of patience: the red
Queen falls on the black King
& the black Jack drops onto
the red Queen, a procedure

I find very encouraging. It
fills me with fresh optimism. But
oh God there is hardly any
paper in here & you are

pinning small birds to the
wall again. One is hanging
on to your wrist & flapping
its wings like an expensive

watch. I'll be out in a
moment. What a delicate business
love is, sweetheart, what
a musical approach to time.

BONES

If I am in your
room I am lowering
the blind.

In the corner
is a washing-machine
full of bones.

You turn on the
light, I light a
candle.

Davidson told me
you know what
to do with your body.

In the corner
is a washing-machine
full of pickled onions.

THE DIRECTORY

When you make
noises you mean that
it doesn't hurt but

I want to
catch you when
you slow

right up. I want
to listen to you, that
needs to be

understood. Meanwhile I
remove the
telephone-book from

the oven and tear it
in half, thinking
goodbye to numbers. The last

discovery is that
the world is so
small, it

contains so many
bodies, filling
with solid light. I

never wanted to
be lucky but
that's how it goes.

THE CINEMA

The Americans make many spectacular movies:
the surroundings of the town are beautiful,
the lake is enclosed by trees.

The other night we went
to a realistic, pitiless film. The spectators
cried, 'Encore!' Afterwards, we felt
we had risked everything.

Early in the morning, we weighed anchor.
We were on board a Russian steamer,
trying to find our sea-legs.

On shore there were many hardened criminals.
Many fields were under water,
many faces lit by summer lightning.

THE PICKPOCKET

We get on well together.
We vie with each other in politeness,
promising no special treatment.
We contradict ourselves constantly.

Look at those people. She leads him
round by the nose, they are always bickering.
He is nurturing a viper in his bosom:
she must have applied for the post.

But, what a day! The favourite lost
by a neck. We lost everything but the clothes
we stood up in! I wish you
good fortune with all my heart.

THE PAPERWEIGHT

The highly prized photograph of the paperweight
The paperweight which has not been placed on paper
But within which snow nevertheless goes on falling
The weight of words on paper
But then of course the weight of paper

The glamorous earth as the sun beats down
The dangerous steps at the entrance to the library
The never-to-be-forgotten day-to-remember
The disreputable restaurant with its intimate charm
In which the voice returns the feathers to the waiter

THE SONG

My body as an act of derision,
eating up the answers to life.
There is the bird-song, now,
elbowing through berries while
the hairs in my nose catch
at the little bits of existence.

And I know you go on living
because you need to be cared for.
I embrace you, I kiss you,
trusting in an ordered development,
watching the small explosions
under your wrists.

Oh we survive merely by good fortune,
by random appetite: going
outside to lie on our stomachs
as if we meant to swim in the earth,
floating near the dazed horizon,
giving this music into the light.

THE DREAM

Lovers, the bodies one by another,
riding their bones into darkness.
If we dream of the man who comes
to the door, offering all
that is profitable, it is only
some means to stop breathing.

We are falling into the earth again,
down the tremendous hole that ends
in China, where by some miracle
we are still on our feet, like trees
dropped out of the sky. Let's build
plantations in China, a world

passing in and out of the world.
Let's inhabit the factual earth

and have small women in our rooms
to wake us, plumping the pillows
we rest our heads on, those
clouds and distant accidents.

CLOUDS

Time is months and your mother's promise
Less than it was
And still you believe it
Less than it was and here it is again

The sun's reluctant to shine so what
It's always exceptional as the clouds go over
It's always better
To swim to the middle of the lake and surface

And immediately you say that
And childhood dies it wasn't murdered
And language is stealing something again
Probably words

Then why is this all so terrific
Why do the clouds go over so high
So high over the tree
And still I can't climb

You don't sleep there but at least you're visible
You don't sleep at all any more
But you can try to go on
You can close up the house and leave it

HOW TO TAKE OFF YOUR
CLOTHES AT THE PICNIC

It is hardly sensuous, but having
eaten all the cold meat and tomatoes
you forget to remove your trousers

and instead skip stones across the river
with some other man's wife
until, finally, the movement

of a small wind, no larger
than the reach of a finger
& thumb, makes it

impossible, carefully lifting off
every item of clothing.
Then you may share an apple and watch

from your side of the river
shoes & socks coming down
to rest on the other.

DEVOTION

Mary, Mary, quite to the contrary
I like you dressed in silk.
This is nearly as difficult as wreckage.

Besides, Mary, it is quiet in the country
and noisy as time passes.
We were all watching your heavenly glances

and loved to be in this forest.
We still like the trees and parachutes.

Century and century, Mary, dances;
then everything departing
There are stars in the wooden slippers
making them heavy.
When we kiss, we have passengers.

THE MUTABILITY CANTOS

1
It's about time I was on time, late
at night, a little unhappy,

endlessly yellow. It's about time
we met, time we went silly,

not yearning, not about to turn back,
at least not this time.

2
Will you tell me? Will you go
out of your way to feel wanted,

taking your time if you want to?
Will you – the tub of cold water

you left out, to fall into love
into – ? It's about time.

3
How nice things aren't the same any more
almost as I like them.

At least *you* remember.
This morning

in particular, the rainfall: the rain
invading under your lashes.

Time after time, downstairs
in the pagoda. Time

after time, out in the garage:
I liked that especially.

4
Mother was present, but not be trusted.
Poor uncle was barely afloat. Indeed,

my late wife had left me, a slight difficulty,
but you remained irresistible.

Time after time,
do you remember?

After the invasion?
Time after time.

5
Time after time, and I told you
it takes time. This morning

especially, somewhere out in the fields,
as good again where the dew

not for the first time
made us helpless; like the last time

I wanted too much of your time
and took it, and time and again

I told that boy,
take it easy, now

take your time, this time
take a little more time about it.

FLOOD

All day I stack cans
of apricots under the stairs:
against the rain flooding
the streets and the people
wading.

Then Melanie calls. It takes
three minutes to speak
to Melanie and to win her.
Later, she tells me her mind
is musical.

A decade of that: and
the storm, myself enrafted.
My proper freedom with apricots,
suspiciously orange and white
as an elbow.

SOME EPITHETS

1
Weary, stale, flat, unprofitable

world:
        hesitation conquers you,
your heart flies up.

What will these words be, without you?

2
What will you be,
what will you be

without those who care, assuming them?
Light, dark, quiet, loud,

soft rotten perfection.

3
Knowledge of them:

those who precede
and those who come after,

those who have knowledge of small flowers
and fall asleep in water

touching the soggy fists:
soaked and glorious, almost prevailing.

4
World, I mean,

world, world, world:
                            I mean
the stars:
            horizons, charts,

the gravel path:
                            your birthdays
on the vigilant water.

THE FRIENDS

Tenacious cries that shake
the heart with low resistance.
The weather is rain we have just
come out of, only to find
the house in fragments,
damaged by song that leaves us

sad. No matter, Señor God,
we're never bitter, planting crops
or growing our moustaches,
celebrating ladies who come by:
enough to tell us life's worthwhile
and getting better.

Tonight, no cloud,
a moon over the river.
We swim out and anchor
in its light. Water that washes us
with song, women drifting
in the rafts of water.

THE COAST

A little is too little, passion
is missing all our fine attention.
We require a nominal vision
to spend the mind on, sound
in its pure circle, the tongue
covered in stars – in that

direction, in *that* direction
it went, and goes. We lack mirrors,
we lack some use in being here
with no one passing by
but signalling a death.
Well, you set sail in your ship:

I set sail in my ship. *Rendezvous*,
in the middle of the ocean,
treading water with a sense
of luminous existence, lips
in an improvised collision,
efficient gift for someone drowning.

THE TREES

Barques we ride on over the sea:
we like to come in on the tide
alone and when it's morning, first
light shattering the bodies.
We want to go under completely,
a well-heeled relic of devotion.

Shapes in the dusk, the faithful
breathing, happens under leaves;
though what does it matter, let's suppose –
'under the circumstances' is where *we* are.
The truth is a requisite urge,
nobody's lover. Sweet sweetheart,

I have a good intention to be better.
I mean to be a silence,
a hair on the floor of the forest.
Why, I sometimes hope to be your pleasure,
the raft you swim out to in lake-water,
shaking a little when your body touches.

CONTEMPLATION OF THE HEAVENS

after Camille Flammarion

Innumerable worlds! We dream of them
Like the young girl dreaming
Who separates with regret from her cradle.
What cannot this adorable star
Announce to the tender & loving heart?

Is it the shy messenger
Of the happiness so long desired?
What secrets has it not surprised!
And who bears malice against it?

And yet, what is the earth?
Is not the great book of the heavens
Open for all to see?
Seek, talk, find out in your conversation.

GOOD LOOKS

THE BREAKFAST SESSION

You want to sing, halfway
up the ladder. Father goes
for a run in the car
looking for what's authentic.
He won't be back,
he's left you to it;
he won't be back for some time
he won't; he won't be long.
And it won't help
to compare her to a flower
whatever sort you hit on
in the course of singing.
You're not a machine
in a bloody paddock
so they say, you don't just
use these things in
evidence. See even here
in the present her eyes
light up with modest pleasure,
yes you don't belong. See
even the cat likes you
which is a start
and not, old son, a hindrance
though its kittens seem
to make it harder.
And the song arrives
with everything complete and heavy,
the sweetness of the air
is not excessive,
nor is it long, and
you really do
appreciate it
and it's not your song.

YOU: A FRAGMENT

1

There must be some remedy for air,
the voice in your chest like water.
There must be some better place
than deep in the body
where only your lungs make you real.
But of course you are valuable.

You put on your coat, you go out,
into the street, and there you are,
unhappy but real among traffic.
If you walk out of here alive,
there you are, *where* you are,
under the stars, still in your body.

2

Gradual eyes, gradual existence,
sleep making you useful.
There is smoke in the flowers
you might enter, a faint bridge
of mist beyond glass where cars
are passing with you in the lead.

Lifted to the spectacle
you cannot watch, but utter
the loud faithful cry and take
breath for the next,
the next best,
then refuse all conversation

3
while we exchange the flower for a flower,
listening for the voice
which we keep company, which
is what we have done,
which is what we were meant for
and certainly all we can do.

A gathering – the sister,
the sister, the brother,
the son, the son,
the wife – ourselves
together.
Then this thought strikes you.

A SONG ABOUT THE MOON

The moon lives by damaging the ocean
The moon lives in its nest of feathers
The moon lives in its nest of clamps
The moon lives by aching for marriage
The moon is dead, it has nothing to live for

The bodies are dangerous, you should not touch them
The bodies resemble our own, they belong together
The bodies are weapons, someone will die of them
The bodies will not lack for wings, someone will find them
The bodies are maimed but you will not remember

Do you still suffer terribly?
Do you always speak French?
Do you stare at the moon for you cannot forget it?
Do you long to be emptied of nothing but feathers?
Do you want to go on like this almost forever?

You must abandon everything after all
You must abandon nothing at least not yet
You must abandon hilarity
You must abandon your flags
You must abandon your pain, it is someone else's

You must abandon poetry for you cannot forget it
You must abandon poetry, it never existed
You must abandon poetry, it has always been fatal
It is like the moon, it is like your body
It is like the ocean, it is like your face

WHAT IT MEANS TO BE NAKED

As you will know
the hands join hands to sing

and then you are naked.
Under the snow, the hands and chest

are draped, and with them the belly;
the thighs are pure bone

sunk without trace. Likewise
the eyes,

the mouth, the nose
sink in the face, while the teeth

are left surprised
by the pain which has vanished.

Also, as you will know,
the tongue leaves

its voice and taste to the snow
and the room at once

grows chilly. The hair,
of course, stays on the pillow.

Then the penis is removed
and shaved, as you will know,

and is buried subsequently
in snow: and this latter,
covering the earth as always,

as you will know,

and being no more
than the usual snow

under the snow
the snow will eat it.

WINGATUI

Sit in the car with the headlights off.
Look out there now
where the yellow moon floats silks across the birdcage.
You might have touched that sky you lost.
You might have split that azure violin in two.

DETTIFOSS

Snow that is late arriving
and like your photograph of snow;
light which chains itself in wings,
light which neglects the water.

GOOD LOOKS

We talk and talk till silence interrupts.
Oh, distance won't harm you,
it's where you belong, where
I first knew you, where you
go on knowing
there is no special relief
because there is no special pain.

What did I think of, thinking
you would wake? What
did I think thought mattered
or what for?
Why do I think you still know better
though I know you are wrong?
Oh, one blames the light, which will not retreat,

one blames gravity for the tree
which is sinking, one blames oneself.
One travels out into the country
and jumps from the tallest tree
blaming the descent on clouds:
and then one falls, knowing
the words not splendid, just pretty.

THE SELENOLOGIST

Is gazing at the moon again.
He stares as usual through his optic lens,
The length of tube with glass at either end.
There, as it happens, is the outside cat;
And there are the fox & the flower & the star.
Among all these his life takes place.

There also is the river of light
Which moves past stars with golden rays
Too bright to contemplate or gaze upon.
The river itself begins in snow,
Far out in space. It travels under cloud,
And those who travel in the boat upon the river

Are pleased to hold beneath the cloud
Because there they are always safe.
(Of course, they will never again traverse
The space they have just left
And which they have just deserted forever,
They will never again embrace brothers or sisters:

They are looking for life on another planet.)
Imagine, before the selenologist was born
They were on their way. They dipped their oars
In cloud and thought of water. Even now
They hardly know if they are touching water
Through the cloud – for they are going with

The current anyway. They are unknown life
But not to each other. They know each other
By their voices and the songs they sing; yet

They can only assume the content of these songs,
The golden stars past which they journey,
They can only assume the water.

This is not strictly true
For they can almost guess at death.
They can imagine the faces, growing older;
Also, they know that if one should fall
From the boat, then it is one voice less;
And yet that such a splashing will confirm the water.

It is then they sing with purest pleasure.
The selenologist can hear across all space
The sound that water makes when violently displaced
And fancies he can hear them singing.
He knows that before he was conceived
This noise was on its way; and smiles

And sighs and gives the cat its supper.
He tells the story of the fox & the flower
& the star, he writes how happy all these are.
He sighs and writes: 'Life is motionless
In consequence of all the time it takes.'
He sighs and writes: 'Distance sets limits

Where our vision fails in space.'
He tries to imagine the boat upon the water
But can see only grass in a small field
By the river at the edge of cloud.
It is immense vegetation, fixed in place:
Green as emerald, soft like a lake.

THE SWALLOW

John Keats,
what is he counting on,
his fingers? No

John Keats is counting on
the morning – the clouds rise
skyward one by one
from all his fingers.

He stands tiptoe
on a little hill.

Oh please
let's be otherwise adequate.
Maybe there *will* be a situation
in which the lot stands revealed,
maybe it's already shaping up,
coming from somewhere
where it once looked good.

We wake at night for example
among the examples. The stars themselves
are full of right results
and cargo, months and months,
day after day just breaking,
each one hoping
to be persuaded it's essential.

And this poem called 'The Swallow',
either it is destined to be purely culinary
or it's about the clear blue sky
which all the birds were leaving.

Never mind, be done with it.
There's always evident progress.
a) The lover makes a loud noise.
b) Then the lover is hidden entirely.

THE BURIED SOAP

Cold spring morning.
All the same

Matthew Arnold's big
silver lips

puff out
their tiny stars:

one there,
one there,

one there,
above the cars.

★

Oh I will simply
stay at home

and ask her
to caress me.

The tiny scratches
on my arm

are quietly healing.
A little heat,

a little pain
and pleasure,

they'll be
gone again.

★

Or I will simply
take some course

of action like
the train

and wash myself
with all this buried

soap. Don't
do it,

writes a friend.
Don't give

up beauty
love and peace nor

yet all hope,
we hope.

★

Well
I could sit

among these loud
white flowers

my friend
possibly for

hours
and endless

hours on end.

★

'So first
it was the trees

went purple then
went green.' Dis-

gusting, how
obscene. I think

that's just a wicked
thing to want

to say, Charlene.

THE IDIOT: A PASTORAL

1
Heavy music: the radio's in love
with old recorded time
and over there they're taking
the mowers
to all the hopeful green stuff.
The bee floats over the map

looking for the last flower,
and thereafter it's cold,
it's bloody freezing.
The chill white flesh drops off
then, look,
all the blades at rest.

2
The poor old bee, alas, is second-best,
unlike the mowers who still affect to live
within those eager formal patterns
which the lovers praised before discarding.
Nothing's secured my love

by what we want, or even what we mean to.
We meant to call, 'Watch out!'
or something like it
but 'knew not' who to call to
(i.e. the bee or the mowers).
At the last

there wasn't an evil man in sight,
and not a wicked woman to be seen.
No witnesses.

And anyway the tree
just lowered its machine.

RIDDLE

The breath still in me,
I go always on foot.
In the green fields, I tear up the earth.

When all life has vanished
I bind fast the dark men of Wales.
Better than these I can tie up in knots.

Sometimes I am the warrior's courage:
he drinks at my belly.
And sometimes the bride places her foot upon me.

Then a Welsh girl, far from home,
swings her dark hair
and holds me close.

Late at night, drinking,
she wets me with water,
warms me with fire.

Her hot hand draws me
over her breasts. As I stroke
darkness, she is writhing forever.

Say me my name.
Living, my wealth is the land.
Dead, I am truly of service.

THE ANGLO-SAXON ONION

1
I am a wonderful creature.
I have a use for those nearby.
I bring joy to women.

2
I harm no one,
only the one
who takes my life.

I am well elevated. I grow tall
in a bed. Somewhere below
I am shaggy.

3
Ah the beautiful girl,
the brave girl, the peasant's daughter!
she risks herself to hold me:

she tears my red skin,
she grasps my head
and clamps me fast.

4
And so she confines me,
this curly-headed woman.

At last she feels
the force of our meeting: ah
ha! her small eye moistens.

WEN

1
Wen, wen, little wen

here you shall not timber
nor have abode

but journey north to the hills
& your miserable brother

he will lay a leaf at your head

2
Under the haunch of the wolf
under the wing of the eagle
under the claw of the eagle
may you sicken forever

lessened like coal on the hearth, burning
like mud on the wall, scraped down

lessened like water, low in the pail
staining the air

3
Be small as a linseed-grain
eaten by worms

& smaller than a worm's hip-bone
dragged under till you are nothing

WULF

1
They take it from me:
            in the manner
of a gift

if danger moves in the earth
is the life given
is it love between us

2
Wulf: on that island
        – I on this other

shut into fens, a bone
in the neck of a savage

if danger moves upon water
is the life given
is it love between us

3
In my mind we joined together:

as it rained, as
I was sad in the rain, as
he laid me with his arms

into his shoulder
a joy given into me like sorrow

4
Wulf, Wulf,
       it is not
at all hunger shaking my limbs
but that you do not journey

       absent & yet
       you fill me

5
They take it from me:
       in the manner
of a gift

the spine of a feather, a cloud in the body

       ai, it is
       easily broken, what

was never at one:

you & I, *Wulf,* the one
with the other

& singing

RIDDLE

Like a dwelling
place, stone upon
stone. Like

rain, slow into
the bark, stone
upon stone.

Like branches, letting
fall, slow
into the bark, stone

upon stone. Like
dust, the hollow
bell, letting fall

slow into the
bark, stone upon
stone. Like

mist among flowers.

VIDYAPATI'S SONG

My lover's limbs are placed
as ornaments.
My lover's ornaments are eyes.

House darkened by lanterns
Moon darkened by hair
Darkness goes out with its voices

My lover's breasts are marked
with nails. Ah see,
her single garment is the rain.

House darkened by arrows
Moon darkened by song
Darkness goes out with its voices

POEM AGAINST THE NATURAL WORLD

Oh star, you are wounded,
oh little pain.

Let us arise, and seek poetry.
Let us gather in a cloud

or rather let us gather
in a cloud of throats
or in the throats of birds.

Oh beaks! Suddenly poetry is a mirror
in which I see an empty cage
and in the cage a few stones.
Suddenly I enter a stone.

At once I am a stone
thrown against the mirror.
At once I am wings.

And I think:
Every night a poem,
every night this terrible wind.

And every night I piss into the wind,
oh little wound, oh remedy.

LOOSENING UP POEM

Loosen up chum. The ocean
spray between coast
& grandfather, between father
& son, doesn't stain anything very
much at all & everyone's either pleasantly
asleep or singing somewhere in the distance.
If the swallows come back
If the wicked Ayatollah
If the bloody airport isn't closed by fog etc
& if the mind (that's what?)
persists in going absolutely blank
& makes the thin blood curdle then run cold
because this time kid you know they're
really coming for you, if the pen
still goes on running out of ink
you know you've seen it
all before, you know
the pressure still indents the paper

LOSS OF THE FOREST

Love is a fact
and black and blue is the skin
of water and sometimes milky white
and the fable always involves a boy with wings
who doesn't care for his biographer
and when the boy comes down to earth
the dogs all run to bite his body.
Here's what to do.
Get in the car and hurtle past the chooks.
Here's what to do. Head for the beach
and sit on the sand till all the people
leave the beach then make
as if to leave yourself. Ah well
at least climb well above the waves
and listen to the little darkness notes
which only sleeping birds outdistance.
Write a song about the wind
and send it to the one you love. The wind
is more important than the forest tra la
though the loss of the forest
would be terrible. Paste some clouds
above the map
and let the wind just puff them out to sea.
Let the ocean liner sail away!
Let them smash the plaster
off your leg with hammers!
And if the boy still yearns to float
then hobble home at once
and tie him to the flagpole
high above the water.

WELLINGTON

It's a large town
full of distant figures on the street
with occasional participation.
Someone buys some shares,
another gets a piece of the action.
Foreign languages are spoken.
A good secretary
is worth her weight in gold.
The man himself
is sitting on a little goldmine.
And down on Lambton Quay
the lads in cars go past, it's raining,
and the boys from Muldoon Real Estate
are breaking someone's arm.
They don't mean harm, really, it's
nobody's business, mainly free
instructive entertainment,
especially if you don't get close
but keep well back like
all the distant figures in the crowd.
So you watch what you can
but pretend to inspect with interest instead
the photographs of desirable private
properties, wondering how close they go
to government valuation. That one's nice.
The question is, do you put your hands
above your head or keep them
in your pockets. Do you want a place
without a garage, could you manage
all those steps. The answer is
the man would simply like you off the streets.
You haven't even got a window
and his is full of houses.

PARTY GOING

It's lonely in the world
when all you get is pity.
The grass is tall and straight
and sometimes waving in the wind.
It grows around the sleeping lovers
and though the police are coming
they somehow look remoter. The last time
I saw you, you said you really
wanted to go home but you had this feeling
you were being followed. You were
half in darkness, half in light,
going outside with all the others.

THE VOYEUR: AN IMITATION

How long a minute seems out in the falling snow
and how pale the late Victorian girl is, sleeping
in her bed. How small she is, the same shade
as the curtains, sahib, sleeping even as she chooses.
We look at her but don't 'relate', living too late
in another century. The lighting is soft and clear
but not intense, like a royal court or the modest glow
or a radio at night and really, she is
somehow medieval, quite flat upon the paper.
And we should put the book down now and just return it
to the shelf and then that way at least
be done with it. But that would be too much like
putting down the ancient family pet, not possible,
even if the mind is gone, the form of what was loved
remains, a passive thing demanding to be cherished.

Also, we have not finished reading. We learned our early
slow advances out of books, getting the answers
off by heart before we knew the questions.
The books showed how the bodies grew
though the books themselves weren't bodies.
We put down other questions and passed them
to the front, and that was reproduction.
The trees we saw were diagrams of trees
with bodies underneath. How far away
those bodies seemed, how cold
they must be now beneath the skies, making
their way through snow by word of mouth
and multiplying as they move towards us. It is
probably their life of whiteness we desire
and probably desire is why you stand
behind the curtains, sahib, and I am here
beside you, persuaded I am also in the picture.
How easily we might partake of what is pallid!
Now you are awake and I am not awake
or I am awake and you are not, and anyway the picture
is a theory: the room itself is luminous.
And we can put this pleasant evening down
entirely to experience, whether or not we find
the girl agreeable, whether we choose to make
advances now or climb back through the window,
postponing the moment once again,
whatever it is we go on imitating.

THE LATE VICTORIAN GIRL

A friend thinks he knows best
and says only because you love him.
And because you make a point of entry
he is grateful and knows where he is
and will do without the usual summary
of facts. Oh he is lost
in the complicated forest of your heart,

he is lost in the forest of your heart
and soon will be obliged to climb a tree and scan
the wide horizon. But it is darker up among
the branches than it is down here, and here
he already knows there is nothing: not the light
of the moon or the light of the stars disappearing,
none of the things he still believes

are needed, not even you.

MAKING HISTORY

The flowers have to be heavy, yes,
and kiss by kiss they knock history
back into the past, they knock it
into little pieces, giving the florist
time to think about a new arrangement.
But first I think
we'll get the new committee round
to watch the light drop through the skylight
and how the leaves land there, also rain,
making that curious effect
we spend all morning staring up at.
That's to say, we'll find a way,
we'll find a way and ever mind the florist.
Also the kisses: the kisses
have to be heavy too, the tongues
gone deep to make connection; they have
to produce that sticky speech
we think we hear the dead ones' voices in.
So now the past comes round again
with all the benefit of doubt
and fails at any rate to penetrate the brain.
But pucker up, the lips are feeling really great
and isn't history the place
where everyone felt great: tired
at the end but not interminable,
under the weather and under the glass,
writing their pleasure into the minutes,
watched by the great big flower arrangements.

THE CARAVAN

Music is this task you undertake.
It is not painful, more like eating crayons
while you lie in bed with the children,
and probably dark in the end
but at least together. Meanwhile
the body waits, delighted to be waiting:
it also cares for the future.

Do you still remember the future?
How it made a lot of noise for instance?
There was a caravan, everyone was travelling.
There were conversations, now ancient history,
in which we hurled the family
from hand to hand and all set out:
or I believe we meant to.

I believe also there were
photographs and flowers, and that when the music
stopped, the children went on singing. Now
the words are largely lost in song, and song is lost
inside the children. We sometimes hear the voices still,
a catch of absence when we sit at table,
crossing that sea on which the facts alone set sail.

MOONLIGHT GOSSIP

Music beats sticks,
the musicians dance in a circle
and their mouths, as they say, bite
the whole of the past, their teeth
clamp hard on memory
as they remember how to do it. *Thud
thuddid*. Hunger respects
a public desperation, and they aren't
above a sort of territorial appeal,
but hunger doesn't want them
that bad – and anyway their hands
aren't beckoning, they clap and clap
and then they're merely
up for grabs. Someone must have
pinned those ribbons to their tongues
so we would all sit late
and watch the whole performance through,
someone must have thought
they should be seen to have them.
And certainly when they yell,
certainly when they *yell*, the whole thing
works all right, the colours flap, the mouths
flap wide with all the colours, the heads
are almost flags, a memorable sight.
All right, you sit late,
you sit and watch and taste the music
and feel convinced the moonlight will improve it.
Thud thuddid and your voice
attempts a low hum
while you think to note the way
a bird refuses to compete
and soaks itself in shadow,

the grass going darker than the empty air
even after the film crew's lights go on
so everything can go on rolling,
and the children come out
from under the trees at last
not as you hoped to start their latest song,
only to make their last appearance.

THE AFTERLIFE

Enormous purple dawns, the water
was always rising, was always
soft and optional and always soft
to enter. I suppose therefore
we entered, believing those dawns
would hardly happen often, not
wanting to let our lives make do.

Of course the world stood still
and all the stars popped out
like baby light bulbs. Of course
the moon would usually come out
and thus improve the view.
Tell everyone, we said. Sometimes
at night I turned to you,

we turned the page, and there was
the yellow forest once again, the corridors
of yellow trees, the bright birds
roaming down. They tossed their frozen
rags towards the sky and still
got stuck in marmalade, still found
they made the usual passage

from aspiration to regret.
Their feathers floated down
all over town. Indeed the afterlife
was all blue sky
with sometimes enormous purple
mornings. The flowers and clouds
which always seemed to sweep

the afternoons were merely
part of the local colour, as also
were the poets, who worked so hard
to scribble down their presence,
who set a furious pace
between the sheets
and wrote their dirty books

to read aloud and grew upset
when no one listened. We
didn't regret regret. We didn't
regret a life of pointless aspiration.
We wrote each other letters
and found our language suffering
from deep concussion

in its deepest structures. Love
was detained by loveliness we thought
like sticky jam, like some accomplishment
we somehow spent our feelings
getting to. Nothing got said.
It was a world of silent pictures,
damp and magical. It was

between me and you and not
between those fixtures. I wanted to write
straight home for instance
and make the big announcement.
You wanted me, I wanted you.
I never wrote the letter.
Each time I tried, the syntax

seemed to rot and leave
a few choice phrases underlined.
And then I supposed no words would do.
There was nothing I thought to say
that sounded true, nothing at least
to write straight home about,
no one at home to write home to.

NIGHT WINDOWS CAREY'S BAY

You write a long poem
about how you are sorting yourself out at last
and how at last you say
there'll never be another word
about departure. Look
around you how the moon
tattooes the spaces all around you,
it isn't even dark. In the house
of doors, the doors are open.
In the house of glass, the glass lets in the light.

RED HORSE

The red crayon makes us
happiest, selected out with care
and making the outline of a horse
when once it's there complete
a rare delightful business;
then colouring the horse in
red as well, occasionally
going over the edge
but mostly filling up the space
without dismay or panic
and reaching in the box
eyes closed for something more or less
surprising for the sky and finding
deepest blue by accident.

DECLINING THE NAKED HORSE

The naked horse came into the room.
The naked horse comes into the room.
The naked horse has come into the room.
The naked horse will be coming into the room.
The naked horse is coming into the room.
The naked horse does come into the room.
The naked horse had come into the room.
The naked horse would of come into the room
again if we hadn't of stopped it.

BREAKFAST

Damp white eggs
which just make Toby sick,
warm tea, a little toast and honey.
Vanessa sits at the table
with her book,
pasting some stars in the margin.

WHEN YOU'RE DEAD
YOU GO ON TELEVISION

Toby lying on the floor
Is really climbing in some tree.
He has no wings, and so he flies.
He has no beak, and so he sings
He has no song, and so he tells us.

POEM FOR VANESSA

1

She wants to fly
Like a big flower floating
Like clouds above the house

She wants to sing at breakfast
She won't eat toast
She wants to catch my eye

And I am writing her
The longest poem in the Southern Hemisphere!
Oh passages of cloud & sky!

2

The longest poem in the Southern Hemisphere
Regrettably, has very little to say
About the Southern Hemisphere

We know that the people
Are small and dark
Dark hair, dark eyes

We know they live in dreams along the coast
They make their small dark noises
And they cry

3
Oh who am I talking to?
That is, to whom am I talking?
Oh, not to you

And not to you:
The longest poem in the Southern Hemisphere
Alas, is not for every eye

Subsequent sections
Shall go directly
to Vanessa, by and by

VANESSA'S SONG

When there's moonlight
on the tussock
I'll be there   (I'll be there)

When there's moonlight
on the tussock
I'll be there   (I'll be there)

When there's moonlight
on the tussock
lighting up your yellow hair

When there's moonlight
on the tussock
I'll be there

CHILDREN

The likelihood is
the children will die
without you to help them do it.
It will be spring,
the light on the water,
or not.

And though at present
they live together
they will not die together.
They will die one by one
and not think to call you:
they will be old

and you will be gone.
It will be spring,
or not. They may be crossing
the road,
not looking left,
not looking right,

or may simply be afloat at evening
like clouds unable
to make repairs. That
one talks too much, that one
hardly at all: and they both enjoy
the light on the water

much as we enjoy
the sense
of indefinite postponement. Yes
it's a tall story but don't you think
full of promise, and he's just a kid
but watch him grow.

LAST THINGS

The kids want to grow up
and be on the phone and everything.
When they throw stones into the creek
they want to make a decent splash,
they want to get that stranglehold
on water. As usual words of praise
conclude the story we were just
beginning to read
but flipped to the end instead:
the family dog was strong and safe
and underneath himself, no one
was lonely. The stone like stone
hit bottom and was obsolete.

AN OUTLINE

First we disowned parents
because they always said *after*,
and friends promised to be around
but were not. Our teachers gave
encouragement and then prescribed
the lonely flower inside the brain.
One showed a picture
but soon would kick the bucket.

At home, away from home, but mostly
nowhere special, we took our own advice.
We got in the car and then just drove
along the road past cliffs and river,
and when we stopped
we slept on the parchment floor,
taking it for the real thing.
We wrote out the poem and slept on it.

Still, there was nothing good for us in words,
or nothing couched in formal English,
while being good itself was good for nothing,
and then again there was always something
coming next, though no particular direction.
The baby lay in its cot and cooed
or it lay afloat in water inside mother.
When once that baby grows, we said,

and put away the car. We built the house then
by the side of the road
at the end of the road beside the river.
Friends came and were welcome

though many failed to make sense
except in pieces, and others
had only rested quietly by mistake.
All day they took their boats

upon the water. We felt alone,
perhaps, but full of promise.
We still possessed the poem in outline,
we had kept some image of the flower in mind.
Now, too, there were provisions, jars of preserves
against the future, photographs to remind
that nothing entered the picture
save cats and children; and the telephone rang

to tell of father's death or just
in other words to ask who's speaking.
We sat by the road and watched
the water tremble as it still stayed perfect.
We woke and slept and that is how
we kept in touch. The children woke in the night
and cried and we sang words to cure.
One crashed the car

and the others soon shot through.
We were young too: we thought
that every goodbye was the last goodbye
and that every last word was made to be careful.
We waved and we waved of course, and now
we find we don't stop waving: believing we see
our life at last, and thinking it over,
knowing how far the road goes home.

ZOETROPES

A SCOTTISH BRIDE

Long division and underprivilege,
sweets in a paper twist; or later,
hiking in the hills, days

like the fizz of flowers in a vase
she carried to a neighbour's house,
a war bride with a photograph of home,

and her own house on a single pulse
of stone, lapped by the tidal starlight.
Whose days were those?

A lit hearth, the flames trod water,
and on the dresser a wedding-cake
ascended like a genealogy towards

the two small figures on the top,
standing beside a silver flower
which gave them back a blurred reflection.

Were those the circumstances
which would have to change? A daughter
rehearsed expressions in the mirror,

choosing the face she might prefer to hold,
another touched the perforations
of a stamp, a profile she was saving.

*You cannot imagine, halfway
across the world*, her father wrote,
the sorrow of the undersigned. Was that her mother

then, who made those numbers on a slate?
Were those her children, almost finished eating,
blowing upon their faces in the spoons?

WATER, A STOPPING PLACE

There are places named for
other places, ones where
a word survives whatever happened

which it once referred to. And there are
names for the places water comes and touches,
but nothing for the whole. A world

released from reference
is travelling away. Its monotones of swell
surround the modest island nation

where a man and woman
lie together by a stream
on a blanket anchored to the grass

by stones. She has turned a radio on
and as their passion comes to rest
she hears the first commercial break

which advertises cereals, then tractors.
Later she walks down
to fill a bottle from the stream

and stands, bare feet on gravel,
meaning to scoop water out of water,
her dress tucked up. It is late

to be changing the topic of a conversation
but she is searching for a word,
something to tell him why he something huge

about devotion, some other sound beyond
this small dark gargle from the past,
not vowel, not consonant, not either.

LEGACIES

It was nothing like a legacy.
We didn't know the word.
We dug a hole and buried things in bottles,

a home-made picture dictionary
and seven orange stamps,
an outline map of land and water,

descriptions of our house and school
and things we did there,
news of those days in which we lived.

We laid them deep because they had to last.
Beings with wings would come
in time to come and dig; curious to learn

how people were in that century before
the terrible years of intergalactic war.
Those bottles won't have floated far

but whatever's there by then
will hardly matter. Something
will have made its way through cork

and hatched, and hatched again.
Grubs which grow wings
or eat dark leaf and wood,

stuff rising to the surface leaving
other stuff behind. Things
that eat things! the sizzling colonies,

the meals of afterbirth and rot.
They've got my drawing of a bicycle,
three syllables above two wheels.

SHE SAYS

She lived there once where you were once,
in coastal light and gusts of stone.
Eventually, she says, you're left alone,
and the place is a gap in conversation.

She says you find things out in words:
the sadness of the emigrating master
is ornament-in-darkness, another sort

of language. The heart might be
a field or river stranded in a window,
someone carving a boat there. Beautiful

people, the landscapes of a friendly land.
The poor are as passionate as charity,
surviving in everything they spend.

THE DISTANCE BETWEEN BODIES

Sheets on the floor, a stick
of lipstick on the table,
bits of coastline almost visible at the window.

The distance between bodies
is like the distance between two photographs.
The star on the boy's chest.
The girl's head resting on the star.

GIRL READING

She overhears the sound of things in hiding.
She bites an apple and imagines orchard starlight.
Each time she licks her thumb, its tip,
she tastes the icy branches,
she hears a sigh migrate from page to page.

ZOETROPES

A starting. Words which begin
with *Z* alarm the heart:
the eye cuts down at once

then drifts across the page
to other disappointments.

★

Zenana: the women's apartments
in Indian or Persian houses.
Zero is nought, nothing,

nil – the quiet starting point
of any scale of measurement.

★

The land itself is only
smoke at anchor, drifting above
Antarctica's white flower,

tied by a thin red line
(5000 miles) to Valparaiso.

London 29.4.81

BREAKFAST

Free headphones all
the way (and dinner, breakfast,
light meal, dinner, continental

breakfast, breakfast)
so that 100 miles out of Bahrain
they interrupt *The Creation*

for a duty-free announcement
and every time the plane
takes off, a steward speaks

of likely rescue: *I have important
safety information I
must tell you.* Fingers of south,

★

the white of cloud,
the trees still blowing inland
from the coast to help you

memorise the exits, and high above
the Bay of Bengal, still waiting
for the drinks trolley, you don't

★

so much look up as down
into the endless depth and blue
of sky, choosing not

to watch Burt Reynolds
in whatever the in–
flight movie is, crossing the tip

of India in broad daylight, and
South East Asia somewhere up
ahead, 'patches of mild

*

turbulence', as the headphones
say, a man bent
retching but apparently all right

while we make a circle over Singapore,
dark pavilions where the space
age glows and hoots

*

like Sydney insisting on
its records, the tallest building
in the southern hemisphere (southern

*

hemisphere! piped music
as we taxi between the backyard
swimming pools – *we think you'll*

agree that our young
colony has come along
well. Well

everything's a possibility, or
so thinks the mind that's (mind
that's not yet quite

★

at home – either we *are* the journey
or just the place through which
the journey passes. Goodbye

London! goodbye Europe! somewhere
between Sydney and Wellington,
somewhere above the Tasman,

★

breakfast is served again (breakfast

★

is served again by
Flight Steward François
Ferrari.

MILKY WAY BAR

OUT WEST

I was riding one of the best-loved horses in the world.
Hither and yon, we went, here and there,
in and out of the known universe.

'There goes Wild Bill,' people said.
'Look at that varmint go!'
There I went.

I went straight to the dictionary
and looked up varmint.
'What's it say?' said a friend. 'What's it say?'

I thumbed through the pages.
'Vermin,' I said, 'vermin
with an excrescent t.'

'Well doggone,' said someone,
and it's true, the dog was gone,
lost in the gulches and the sages,

leaving just me and the horse,
a couple of ornery critters
who might just as well mosey along,

crossing the ford by starlight,
and miles away, the woman –
lonely and beautiful – waking to find us gone.

MAGASIN

I have brought my father
things to read, *Pix*, *Post*, *People*,
and I tell him how *magazine*

is like the word for shop
in French. I have just started high school,
I am learning a language.

My father lifts his striped
pyjama top so I can see
what looks like the map of Africa

where the doctor has traced
the shape of his liver
for the third-year students.

At the end of the ward
men are listening to the races
and from the next-door bed

the man with one leg,
the bloke my father says
might have to lose the other,

leans across to tell my father
something about
the second leg at Trentham.

JALOPY: THE END OF LOVE

Do you drive an old car?
Or a jalopy?
Now where could that word come from?

Somewhere in the world
someone you know
must be driving a jalopy.

As for you, one day you are out
on a country road
miles from the sort of place

that might be miles from anywhere
and your car breaks down.
Well, it's an old car.

And somewhere in the world
someone you used to love
has that ancient photograph of you

sitting behind the wheel
high on the Coromandel.
It's a jalopy.

Just at the moment though
it doesn't want to start.
Whatever it is, it's finished.

FACTORY

Thank you, she said, we'll stick
to our current satisfactions, thank you
I'll thank you

to speak when you're spoken to.
Oh such chilly rehearsals
chill you to the bone. Halfway

across the busy road,
halfway home, full of the repetitions
which are yours alone,

you remember what she told you,
years ago, you were talking
of this and that,

exchanging pleasantries,
and you said this
and she said that, and then . . .

Strange how the memory soothes,
so easy and quiet, yet still in touch
with spite. It brings you back

to the fact of the matter.
It brings you back
to the place of manufacture.

MILTON

Someone leaves *Paradise Lost*
on the photocopier. Every so often
an experimental policeman

will make a note or two
then take the weekend off.
That's probably how it was

with Milton. He walked along
the long, long line
wondering who was supposed to be guilty.

No one prepared him for this.
He didn't know about guilt and innocence,
he didn't know about Milton.

All of those people,
all of them living at this hour,
all staring away somewhere . . .

He looked at the man with the scar,
the weeping woman,
the pustular pair holding hands.

He chose the hand-holding couple.
Why? Because he was lonely,
because they were there at the end.

SOUTH ISLAND COMPANION

Kaikoura, Bluff, the Haast:
places go by, and that's how
you leave the past, not even

alphabetical order. And wherever you stop
you say: Do you think
things happened here?

On the coast road
between Warrington and Karitane
the screech of wheels brings to mind

the girl in the car: angel child
whose wings bring to mind
the body between them.

Question: Was she
more alive than you are now?
Were you more alive

than the fact of her beauty?
Oh better go on, better
find something to drive you along

and a new road
on which to be careful.
Then Dunedin approaches:

you drop down
to roofs and that gray
documentary harbour. Twilight is there

and one wee sail,
and the car just goes on
taking the corners. You lean across

to the life in the throat
below her smile and hear
how the city Dunedin

seems to fail . . . note
after note after note
of the Richter scale.

OUR FATHER
for Charles Causley

On one trip he brought home
a piece of stone from the river,
shaped like a child's foot

and filled with the weight
of the missing body. Another time
he just walked in

with our lost brother
high on his shoulders
after a two-day absence;

and it seems like only yesterday
he was showing us
the long pole, the one

out there in the yard now,
taller than twice himself,
that still hoists

our mother's washing out of reach.

MILKY WAY BAR

I live at the edge of the universe,
like everybody else. Sometimes I think
congratulations are in order:
I look out at the stars
and my eye merely blinks a little,
my voice settles for a sigh.

But my whole pleasure is the inconspicuous;
I love the unimportant thing.
I go down to the Twilight Arcade
and watch the Martian invaders,
already appalled by our language,
pointing at what they want.

MASTURBATING

Poor boy. Here he is,
home from Bible Class.

He closes the door.
He lifts the mattress
and takes out the book with dog-eared pages.

Whenever I think of him,
I half remember Gaynor
who used to go out
with the local stock-and-station agent.

She was a teacher
but she couldn't spell –
a girl from Christchurch
doing her country service.

She said the trouble was
she took after her father
and he was a bit touched.

For example, she could remember
when she was a child.

'Here is the church,' he would say,
'and here is the steeple;
open the door
and there are the fingers.'

MY LOST YOUTH

'My lost youth
as in a dream,'
begins this poem

beginning with a line
in what I think is Polish

★

glimpsed

on a sheet of paper
in the ticket-office
at the bottom of the cable car.

Two men behind glass
are bending over it,
the careful, mysterious

copperplate of Polish,
the English lightly
pencilled in above . . .

Of course there is more to it
than my lost youth,

★

patches of pain and love,
a page from start to finish,

148

but you can hardly go on looking,
and tourists are lining up

★

and someone punches
your new downtowner

and through you go
and leave the poem behind –

keeping in mind a phrase or two
as you travel backwards up the hill

★

to alight at last

above the wooden town
they've nearly finished tearing down
to make the city . . .

★

something about desire perhaps,
something about desire,
the fears . . . or fires . . . of youth,

★

'her mortal gown of beauty' . . .

MISCARRIAGE

In the year most of the girls
started wearing bright colours,
my youngest daughter wore gray.
She sat up late, reading the paper,
nursing her terrible temper.

A lot of it slips
my mind now, but one night
her beauty slowly dawned on me;
then dawn came too
and her place was empty.

Where had she gone?
Was she lost in the headlines?
I think she must have slipped out
while I was reading something
over her shoulder.

EARLY DAYS IN THE COLONY

A whole row of bibles.
A page about being frightened.
They took off their clothes
in pines above the bay.

And all the time she kept talking
(but nothing he proposed to understand)
about which one it was
should be minding the baby.

So she was adrift on the shapeless day
(and there were no pines
except in the miserable background
and in the foreground only trouble)

her face as white as a seasick girl,
her voice like waves at sea.

BEACH LIFE

Early morning, there's

a slice of light
(electric) beneath the door,
someone going along

the corridor. The baby's
asleep between sheets
of pale blue water

while outside a tractor
tows the first boat
down to the beach.

In the next-door
room and nearly
dressed, you're reciting

an early twentieth-
century poem – benign
neglectful cadences, still

pining to go home.

ONLOOKERS: A STORY

The plastic bags
are filled with water
and the small bruised fish

swim there, swung from hand
to hand above the footpath
like the lyrical bits

towards the end of chapters
plagued by the great outdoors: there
above and beyond them are

the wide blue streets without function,
the rambling man who suddenly remembers
his address minus, alas, the name

of the relevant city. He is probably not
inside anything, this man, not even
a story. Probably the action

includes him just to spit him out.
He turns to the world and starts to shout,
something about language or a living wage,

while the untrained reader turns the page
to find the day beginning
cold and safe again. The house

is packed with vacancy
like a fortune-teller's scarf
immense with rain. Parents

spell words across
a table, a mother says quietly
that she couldn't say,

there's nothing wrong. Breakfast.
The children chant *Headlands*
heartlands lowlands

high! and the lonely
room records them
like a song.

AGITATED NATION

1
Words touch the tongue
and there is a man who writes them down.
He says them aloud
and another man watches over his shoulder
to check the spelling.

2
That is how things get done
in the capital city.

3
And the girl herself is always pretty.

She is like rain (he writes)
forgetting what she touches,
the metal roof, the earth, the ocean
still drifting in every direction.

So here is the rain again, falling
on the railway tracks, the lines and sleepers,
on the clattering wagons,
and the red bells of the level crossing.

4
Well done, says the man
who writes words down. And the other man,
the one watching over
the first man's shoulder, decides it is safe
to leave the room for a moment.

He comes back buttoning up his fly,
smiling a little, he won't say why,
humming the song's rotten chorus.

A WINTER CHRISTMAS

Our flat's attacked by tinsel. It steals
across the walls, clinging
by tiny pads of blu-tac. A silver
caterpillar eyes the African violet
while its phlegmatic cousin creeps above
the McCahon poster we've carried all the way
from home. *Tomorrow will be the same*
but not as this is. Out on Gray's Inn Road
they're digging up the road. Pneumatic drills
stutter below our vase of winter daffodils,
snow falls but apparently won't settle.
All day pigeons fly in and out
of the upper windows of the Royal Free Hospital,
and late at night you sense a hint of wind,
probably some stars. The various sounds
of ambulance and fire drift up . . .
A voice or two, one calling *police*
or *please*, then footsteps vanishing.
Dark night, dark traffic, probably some stars.
England alone with her memoirs,
reading the children off to sleep.

BREAKING THE HABIT

Even the children lend a hand,
stealing from room to room,
wrapping your smoke-rings in a towel.

SYNOPSIS (HANDEL'S *IMENEO*)
for Peter Walls

Since a Handel opera consists of a succession of short scenes,
any detailed synopsis tends to be confusing to read. As the
action unfolds on stage, however, it is perfectly easy to follow,
provided that one identifies the characters and bears in mind
their basic aims and attitudes to each other.

Disguised as women we at last drop anchor;
then we herd the ladies back to Athens
where all the senators are stunned and hurt . . .

But this is not Toronto, why have the pirates
entered our conversation? Are they trying
to restore romance or do they want

to leave us in confusion? Any one of us
might be the father of Stephanie's baby.
You know how it goes: you fall in love,

you fall to the floor (oh cruel misfortune),
and by the time you are lifted to your feet
you have become the understudy,

you are just another little ship
drifting towards the Saturday matinee
and in the end you retain your misguided

sense of duty but that will never
see you through. Turn up the stereo,
it speaks not for itself

but for a friend; it sings
through speakers while we can only speak
through song. Meanwhile

things go from bad to worse for Tania
and Ken finds that the horrors of jury duty
are not yet over. Then during the interval

Kate decides to tell the truth – or does she
know about her uncle's ultimatum? Why
is the chorus offstage playing cards?

Why do we rise so often
to applaud the absence of a plot? Spurned
and unrequited! poor Clomiri, rebuked

and beckoned by the music,
and tuned to the contrasting angels
(the one called Sorrow, the one

called Amorous Intention) who hover now
above the darkening orchestra. Perhaps
they are friends of the conductor.

Theirs is the language
of the wild and stormy heart. (We hear
and misinterpret, then depart.)

ALLEN CURNOW
MEETS JUDGE DREDD

How pleased we were, wedged solid,
exhausted forty years ago. Was that
perhaps part of our appeal? We missed

the electroflare, of course.
But all suggested we continue
where we soon left off. Just nod for yes.

The time you rang the doorbell
confirms the sort of feeling
I've been feeling, just

nod for yes. But that's
my feeling, not yours: more than
one poet

got lost in thought
in time long past, perhaps wedged solid.
And electroflare stuff still gets into print,

though neither here nor there. Well
who would contradict? I suppose
we're thinking of the whapp! market

and the whapp! product, I rather hope
the dog is still around. But
it can't be helped, hold

it right there! the best
electroflare poets still remember
something, still find things

a little to their liking.
Now be quiet, I am a limbo wraith
and I want some of your people.

Don't think permanence is easy:
sometimes the marks
are more or less

unmistakable, sometimes they belong
to those who just fulfil
their missions. You expect the firmament

to fail, you expect the raw
mental power of a new
Blast Barclay – did you read

his last collection? But one doesn't
have indefinite time – nod for yes,
shake for no, hold it right there.

I was wedged solid
from the start. I started
by writing something down.

LIFE WITH MADAME ROSA

'Make sure your crystal ball has batteries in it . . .'

1

You never could resist
an invitation to the Fun Fair. You just
love all the excitement of the big
dipper, bumper cars etc.
On one of your many visits there
you notice a good looking boy
selling tickets at a shooting range.
You just keep spending your money there.
When you have no more money left
you find you have fallen in love with him.

2

I see a ring. It has a large
diamond stone. It is not yours.
It is in a shop window which you pass
each morning on your way to school.
Your dream is to have that ring.
One day as you stand looking at it
you hear the voice of a man
who asks you whether you would like it
to be yours. You are scared
and walk off but the same evening
the ring arrives at your house
in a tiny envelope. You never
find out how it got there
or who the man was.

3
Soon after you marry
you have a dear little baby boy.
Your husband is not earning much
and you have to give up your job
and your flat is small
but you both love the child
and he is jolly and easy, you do not
mind working for his sake.

4
I see snow and you have fallen a long way.
Your skis have fallen off
and you are stuck in deep snow
unable to move. Someone comes to you.
He is strong, good looking.
He lifts you up
and gets your skis back on.
You ski off together.
He could be your future husband.

5
One day
you are left a farm by a remote cousin.
At first you are rather horrified at the prospect of farming
but you try the life for a year,
it is fun and useful and you decide
to make it your career. Your friends
and relations love staying with you.

6
You are very fond of animals,
especially rare animals threatened
with extinction. Late in your life
you will become involved
in a movement to preserve the tiger.
You will become very famous.
People throughout the world will be proud of you.

7
You go big game shooting in India.
One day you lie for hours
hoping for a tiger. Quite suddenly
a huge tiger appears apparently
from nowhere and stares straight at you.
He is so magnificent you forget to shoot
and the next moment he is gone.
You are not at all popular.

8
Many years from now
you will live in India. Your job
will take you for long hikes
through the jungle. On one of these
you come across a tiger cub.
You bring up this cub in your home,
he is small and loveable
and you love him like another human being.
When he is barely one year old
he will go back to the jungle
and lead his own life there forever.

9

I see a place of great excitement.
I think it is a fun fair, there
are lights and crowds of people.
I see you there but you are unhappy.
You have lost your purse with all your money
and cannot have much fun.
But somebody has seen your plight.
He comes to help you, he pays
for both of you, you both
have fun. There is always darkness
for the Queen of Hearts
but he could be important in your life,
the future tells me
he could be the one.

Note: Madame Rosa *is an English children's toy: a battery-
operated crystal ball which is accompanied by a book of
predictions. The poem is composed of extracts from the various
predictions. The instruction book includes the following salu-
tary advice: 'Remember always that nobody wants to hear a
fortune of gloom and misery. Disappointment, hardship and
sadness are part of life, but are usually overcome, so make any
sad stories end up happily. This is what people like to hear
and you want a satisfied customer in the end, don't you?'*

AN EXTENDED FAMILY

An uneventful day. When his mother had
one of her attacks, there was a sound
like television in a distant room,
the viewers shifting in their seats,
the channel being changed. Come to that

he sometimes watched television himself,
though only for 'something else to do',
it wasn't so important really. After
some time his mother shifted in her seat
and sang her several songs, one for luck

and one for darkness, and then that longer one
with funny words we never could
make out. About that time night fell
and we all went through to watch it happen.
Yes it makes you happy and it makes you think,

knowing you are loved! like an ornament
the owner kisses every night before retiring:
expensive or valuable or both. We thought
we saw a heap of bedclothes, we heard
her chuckling as she cleaned her teeth.

HURRICANE

I am a poor man
but once I was rich.
Aha! Ho ho!
Now I am dirty, full of itch.
Aha aha aha!

The hurricane came.
It blew away wife (alas),
children (alas)
and then it took
all of my money. Aha! Ho ho!

The hurricane came.
The hurricane came.
It blew away servants:
the ugly and beautiful ones,
each of the sisters and brothers.

Alas all my servants,
the ugly and beautiful,
where are you now?
You are somewhere over the sea,
on an island you cross in an hour.

I hear how you sing now of me,
and you polish the tables
while guests sit to eat
(aha!) the same food
without any flavour.

PRINCESS: THE TREATMENT

She lives behind the waterfall.
Her lords are gone, and she yells
at the few remaining servants.
One day she stands in the mouth of the cave
and says: I've had enough.

Ordinary folk have fled to the woods.
Deep in the swampy forest
they hang their washing on the trees.
The language there means nothing:
Only a princess speaks it.

For example, a crow is not a cloud,
but only a princess knows the difference;
she puts crows in one place, clouds
in another, both in the sky
above some distant province

where darkness has gathered
and perhaps it will soon be raining.
Oops! She claps her hand to her mouth.
Only a princess knows the language.
Our task is to find her.

Well, yesterday we saw a girl in the river.
She screamed when we dragged her from the torrent;
and when we laid her on the bank to dry
she raged and raged and went on screaming.
Was she a princess? We forgot to ask.

And today there are soldiers on the roads,
while tomorrow we leave with the gold.
Wh-wh-what'll we do if we're captured?
You can hide a stone among stones.
But where do you hide a princess?

The princess runs ahead on her powerful
and attractive legs. The rebel governor
stares through his window at the smoky rain.
Tomorrow he must execute the princess.
The rain falls on the firewood where she is hidden.

The great door of the prison rasps open.
All right, he roars, which one of you
is the princess? And we all cry,
I'm the princess! I'm the princess!
So they march away Humboldt the Thing.

Poor Humboldt. But at least the princess lives.
She reaches the city across the water,
or gallops to the safety of the woods.
Then, at the end of the film, when the film is over,
she runs right out of the preview room

crying: This time I'll kill that fucking director!
No, we call, no princess, please don't go;
or rather, let us come with you!
Then we race to the screen
and claw our way up the credits . . .

And there is the princess, at the top!

HIROHITO

I am like a canary whose cage has been
opened and someone says: 'Fly away!'
Where should I fly to? If I have a song
to sing, why should I waste it on places
where the wind may blow it away?

To improve his eyesight
the young Hirohito gazes
at the horizon every day.

Birds and clouds: one day
he will be a living god.

*

In the playground
he always has to be leader;
the other kids
line up behind.

Already he knows
about physical fitness,
the importance of the will.

He likes insects, plants and butterflies.
He admires
the delicate protocols of Nature.

*

One day his father went mad:
he peered at his people

through the paper telescope
of his own speech.

Hirohito watched his father
being taken away
and thought of jellyfish.

★

At the age of 20
he travelled to Europe.

In London he sat for Augustus John.
He played golf
with the Prince of Wales.

In Paris his knowledge
of European military history
amazed the generals of France.

The happiest days of his life.

Hirohito went home to Japan,
ate eggs and bacon,
and dressed like a Western gentleman.

★

Then there was the war:
about which we know the truth
or do not know the truth,

in which Hirohito either played
the leading part
or he did not.

Perhaps he was
just a puppet of his warlords.

Or perhaps they lined up behind him
while he stared at the horizon

and the sun rose
and the sky filled with planes.

★

Hirohito knew everything
and nothing. 'Let the cry
be vengeance!' cried the allies.
'If you meet this man, don't hesitate.'

Hirohito hid inside the palace air-raid shelter,
a bank vault
with ten-metre thick
ferro-concrete walls.

★

When he announced the surrender
his ministers wept:
the god's voice
being broadcast on the radio.

At first no one could understand Hirohito.
He spoke a language of his own.

And for two days the nation wept –
long enough to let the Emperor's chamberlain

replace the bust of Napoleon
in his study

with one of Lincoln.

*

They say that when he met MacArthur
Hirohito bowed so low
that the handshake took place
high above his head.

So the Son of Heaven was a family man after all –
not in the least divine,
just a quiet marine biologist
able to sign the instruments of surrender.

*

I am writing my book about him,
A Modest History of the Wind,
but I am in difficulty:

chapter after chapter
is being blown away.

There he is: the warrior on a white horse –
blown away.

And there: the Shinto priest
planting rice seedlings
in the palace gardens.

Gone.

And look: there is Hirohito
winding his Mickey Mouse watch.
Tick-tock: the wind takes him.

Petals blown away —
as in a haiku,
as in a tanka.

    ★

In this final chapter, a funeral:
the powers of the world
have gathered in mourning.

Hirohito —
the 124th occupant
of the Chrysanthemum Throne.

Glancing idly at the news
I catch sight of him through snow,

a man with glasses
staring out of the screen
of my 14-inch Sanyo.

BRAZIL

1

All night Brazil approached you through the dark.
The light behind mountains
was the light in the silver-merchant's eyes
two villages down river, was the blade
his father's father gave him, years ago,
to help him strike a deal with strangers.
His great right arm struck you
once, struck you twice,
because you had no money.
He watched you walk towards Brazil.

Brazil was women buying food from men,
the directions water followed.
Brazil was stars above the water-raft,
the parchment and the livestock where you slept,
and in the morning you woke and travelled on,
Brazil was where you were going.

Years later, a thousand miles away,
the place was still Brazil,
was still a single-minded journey,
the turmoil of a single coin ungiven,
the silver there in your hand.

2

The people of the second river
announced themselves by clapping;
you entered every village to applause.
You filmed their dances, the bodies
moving to the sound of waterfalls
a little way downstream. You watched

their life go on by word of mouth.
The dance of men with cattle,
of manioc and chicken, the dance of Elvis,
the dance of cattletrucks and pastry.

*

The boy turned to the Senator.
One thousand feet below the copter
you could see the white flashing of water
mixed with the bright grins of bandits.
'Bad country,' he said. 'Poisonous spiders.'

3
Papers on a desk, a river,
and around each bend in the river
Brazil replaced Brazil.
It was a funny idea, she thought:
tampons in the jungle.

Papers on a desk safeguarded the desk.
You sat in a chair while the man there
told you his problems: no village,
no machinery, no available women.

*

The captain sat in his chair while the man
told him his problems. Outside
engines shunted in the yard.
Brazil was several photographs of feathers.
Brazil was urgent measures, which ended
when we disappeared from sight. And around
each bend in the river, Brazil replaced Brazil.

You looked at your ticket: the picture
of birds, the single word, *Brazil*.

4
Take-offs and delays.

Brazil was a rough airstrip in the jungle.
Near the runway, parrots chattered on a log.
He watched the woman spray her hammock
with insecticide, and sat beside her as she slept.
She tossed and turned in the black waters
and white waters of her sleep, imagining
an angel made of bricks. The colonel
came down the path towards them,
already screwing the top off the bottle.
This was more like it! Manioc and chicken
and, if they were lucky, ice-cold lager.

The suitcase was filled with batteries.
Mr Sunday sang on the radio,
a girl waved her Davy Crockett hat.
The explorers sprayed their hammocks
hoping to get a good night's sleep.
Short powerful men demanded cigarettes.
Nose flutes, necklaces of teeth.
She kept glancing at their genitals.
What would she do with so many nose flutes?

She sprayed her hammock with insecticide.
This time, surely, a good night's sleep.
'I'll just knock on the door,' he said.
The senator himself answered, delighted to see them.
Before they were seated, he had taken
the top off the brandy.

5

The secret tribe knew a secret tribe
but would not say. 'Do you mean deeper
in the jungle?' he demanded, beginning to get angry.

But they would not say. The woman
swam, anyway, not caring about the crocodiles.

Butterflies settled on the old Vauxhall Velox.
The word for the snakes was viridescent.
She worried about their driver's bandaged hands.

6

God floated above the Amazon.
He dreamed of Europe under sail.
He thought of the pre-Columbian sky,
and Portugal with cities in its stomach.
He placed a conference of spiders on the track.

★

Brazil, he wrote, was tribe after tribe
attached to stone, windows which rose
above the poverty of beef, everyone eating.

And everything you admired, the people
gave you. This child, this river,
all these trees.

7

'So many birds and I yearn to see seagulls.'
She wrote such things in her diary.

Brazil was the way
her memories all deserted her
and then came back, frightened,
full of apology, asking to stay.

★

Oh her eyes are black, far down,
like stones below a bridge.
Her hair is long, or short,
the way hair is . . .

★

'Can you imagine
this place?' said the young American,
who already thought he would stay.

He turned off the radio.
'It's like there are 500 words for jungle
and only one for flame.'

The man at the FUNAI post nodded.
He went on reading Shakespeare.

8
Brazil would watch the jungle murder sleep
and then perhaps sing on.
Brazil was happy, Brazil
was the great intolerable lines of song
a peasant offered on a piece of stone.

★

Look! They watched
the canoe sing on through the foaming waters.
God was on fire above the Amazon.

★

'There is a place,' sang Mr Sunday,
'beyond the barricades of stars . . .'

★

He turned off the radio
and gave the boy the two batteries.
Muito obrigado. He spoke some Portuguese,

but probably he would never understand
the music he held there, just for a moment,
in the palm of his hand.

9
We filled the suitcase with cigarettes.
The Indians ran towards us.
The Amazon flamed and we shielded our eyes.
The water foamed, it wandered
like the edges of lace, it travelled across
the high wide cheekbones of our race.

★

'Help, look at the time,' said the missionary.
He turned on his heel and was gone.
So this was Brazil.
He stepped out of Brazil, or into Brazil.
He stepped out of the half-built cathedral
and simply vanished into the jungle.

PHAR LAP

Unlikely combinations,

Prayer Wheel and Winkie, Sentiment
and Radium: names that contract and expand
like a big heart pumping

till you get an unlikely starter,
this chestnut colt,
foaled in Timaru, October 4 1926,

by Night Raid out of Entreaty,
with Carbine somewhere
in the background.

*

The hide is in Melbourne,
the heart in Canberra.
The bones are in Wellington,

the big delicate skeleton
of a horse
who used to mean business.

*

Can the name
have been planned as a pun?

In English it is one thing.
In Siamese, Lightning.

And they say it means
something in Egyptian.

★

But he was virtually unbeatable,
the big fellow,
winning race after race in Australia
and never fading,

even after they shot at him,
even after they missed,

★

even after he died in America
of intestinal tympany,
of theory after theory . . .

They say that for five days he ate
pasture sprayed with lead arsenate,

they say that his Australian strapper
gave him Fowler's Solution,
incorrectly mixed,

or maybe even the Mafia . . .

Well, let's say he died in California,
let's say he died of absence

★

and that when they stopped talking
they sent him home,
made him articulate
bone by bone

*

till one day up at the Museum,
it might be fifty years later,

wandering along
past the days of pioneer settlement,

I walk past Cook's cannon
and a case of muskets

and hear a woman sing
in another language

from the far side of Phar Lap's ribcage.

MY SUNSHINE

THE ADVENTURES OF HILLARY

Hillary frowned impatiently.
He'd go ahead with his own plans!
Apricots, dates, biscuits and sardines:
then he donned his three pairs of gloves.

He stamped around muttering
feeling his heart lurch like a vehicle
halfway down a crevasse.
'If, if, if,' he added grimly to himself.

So December came in a rush;
the dog teams fanned out across the snow
barking a bit at the short Polar summer,
while he fretted in his tent, or leant

on his pick and frowned at the pack-ice. If, if, if,
if only the blue skies and breeze
of his father's bee farm, that billy of smoke
where the hills soar up forever . . .

till finally the yak-shepherd grinned and spoke
and they strolled over to where
the sherpas sat by the tidy tents of the Swiss.
Everest! and later he recalled

staring along the line of the Scotsman's finger
to the strange taste of mint on the summit,
while a thousand halls filled for the lecture,
chairs in the soft gray air.

SOME SCREENS

Japanese Pavilion
Los Angeles County Museum

Palace scene in downtown L.A.
Palace scene in a snowy landscape,
spring cherry, autumn maple.

We stand for a while and watch the snow:
the bridge at Uji crossing from spring to winter
each day since the seventh century.

The calligrapher walks in the country
in the golden age of Japanese screen painting.
Nowhere to sit, just the slow, cool spiral,

carp on a hanging scroll,
plum trees and pine, the privileged light
turning gold in the distance

while guards guard the water.
Look, there's a phoenix. And at last
someone's sweeping away the leaves,

the one happy man at the shrine . . .
Such heat! Such snow! Such terrible
traffic! And there's the sad poet

alone in the palace,
there on the fan, a small breeze
that once touched the lady.

REMARKABLES

for Janet Frame

Mountains in boxes,
years of people.

And then she smiles.
'Let me look.' Look up

and over and under
while the blue apple-paper,

the peaks and snow, those
eyes that still gaze and water

once again
get themselves ready.

ISABELLA NOTES
for Harry Orsman

Isabel sits in her study
with a book on her knee.
What a good student: she's looking
herself up in the O.E.D.

Something's on her mind. Quick!
call a lexicographer! Her face
goes gray, then yellow.

She calls for help
¡Socorro!
and the book falls to the floor

oh, and we look up *yellow*
only to find the dirty sheets of paper,
the layers of calico

left by the tired Spanish princess.

★

The lexicographer came to my studio.

I was still working at my portrait of the Spanish princess, the one you will know, which is now so famous. I remember the particular afternoon well. It was gray outside and I was pleased with the cheeky little nose, the way I had caused the light to slip across it, making the lady somehow less severe. Ah yes, he said. Though just a little, he said, I'm not even sure if I should say this . . . just a little . . . but then I suppose it would be patronising *not* to say it . . . just a little more *Isabella* here!

★

Isabel, three syllables,
or four, *Isabella*, a village
between two castles, each

high on its hill, and the light
still there in the evening
when she rides out on her favourite horse,

the one that is pale, its mane
like the snuff-coloured moth
whose wings shiver

at the dark sound of *guitar*.
One day Granada will fall,
one day it will be all

Isabel and Ferdinand
and God: Castile this side
of the ruined wall, on the other

Alhambra, and the artist painting
the girl's face, a mist
in front of the eye, children at school,

all things bright, and beautiful.

★

Isabella: A Game

The centre child pretends to be weeping; another child stands outside the ring and goes to it; when the two meet they kiss.

Then all the children sing:

Isabella, Isabella, Isabella,
farewell!

Last night when I departed
I left her broken-hearted.
Upon the steep mountain
there stands a young man.

Who'll you choose, love?
Who'll you choose, love?
Who'll you choose?

*

Isabelita

When he woke up, the angel said, he felt as if he had slept the night in a suitcase, and that the suitcase had gone as unaccompanied baggage on some considerable air-journey – say, Auckland to L.A. – and had sometimes been upright, sometimes on its side, tucked in the belly of the plane, *above clouds*, then just going round and round on the baggage carousel. There was a man he must have passed a dozen times; the man had a tartan shirt, he was big and bearlike, and he kept saying to the woman with him, 'Christ, where is that bag?' The woman, who was got up in an attractive yellowish-gray

shift – almost angelic, thought the angel – was saying some-
thing about the sea. Perhaps: 'It looked a little askew. Away
down there. Are you listening to me, Hugh?' Or perhaps
something else entirely. Anyway, she seemed meek but
powerful, full of patience. From the duty free the angel could
hear someone saying: 'Do you have obsession? Do you have
eternity?' Eventually the man turned to the woman and said:
'Listen, Isabel. Don't talk like that. Let's lay a complaint and
just get on to the hotel.' But Isabel, if that was her name,
said: 'No, I think we should wait.'

★

Isabel eating an apple
is impossible. The old
apple tree is dead, lost

at the moment when
it was pushing out
the first new blossoms.

The birds sit there, anyway,
black in the branches,
while Isabel, indoors,

inspects the wooden bowl
and takes one peach, then
another, then several grapes.

★

Now she stands at the walls
of the reluctant city.
She smiles as they talk

of the dazzle of Allah.
Now it rains and men
raise a canopy. Now

it rains. The rapture of patience!
She waits in the rain.
Pale calico. She sees

an ocean, pigeons
high in the stone. The edge
of the known world. She is a bridge

extending the edge.

★

The dangerous likeness of Jezebel . . .

★

She lies between the sheets,
a gray woman eating grapes
in the gray mists of the lowlands.

Only the pillow is real
and the chuckle
of hair on the pillow.

Oh my beloved, Infanta!
each brushstroke
makes you more pale . . .

Only lonely
when we can see you. Only
the last only child . . .

While the good folk of Flanders
bring her grapes, the kind
which grow in North America.

All day she stares at them in the bowl,
large bunches of colour:
sometimes green and red,

sometimes that continental purple.

★

The little man was standing outside the lexicographer's house again. He had this big cardboard box of Korean Isabellas, and I suppose he must have been waiting for the rain.

★

'Ariosto loved her, Shakespeare
and Keats, Molière and Dryden,
Marston, Webster . . . And she's a fruitful

extensively forested place in Luzon,'
the lexicographer said,
or just about managed to say

before everyone left the room.

★

A Wee Spell

Ariosto had an Isabel:
he himself isn't known
but the machine suggests *artiest*.

For Keats it offers *cheats*.
Shakespeare's not there,
but his adjective is.

Ostend produces a hothead,
Granada a grandad.
Molière is noisier.

As for Isabella, the system
has no alternative. But put Isabel
under a spell, under a spell-check,

and the machine's dictionary,
which knows inquisition,
goes right past *infidel*

to give *Israel* real quick.

*

Evening sky:

the colour is yellow, gray,
sky sliding against the sky,
the girl hopping into bed

with a parent, a grandparent, a brother,
the smallest one in the family
(he is little, he is simple)

who sees her coming but
oh he cannot
say her name.

★

Isabel, Lisbet, Helsa . . .
I hunt for you in the alphabet,
in the thin, miserable

chambers of the heart, in all
of the pages turned by history: there's
the first place in the new world,

puzzled Columbus, the blustering
crops of corn and tobacco,
extensive forests now abandoned . . .

★

a snuff-coloured moth,
an angelfish, a bear,
grapes, red bay, a children's game:

a kind of whitish–yellow–dingy,
a kind of peach, a pigeon,
a dull straw colour signifying beauty.

MY SUNSHINE

He sings you are my sunshine
and the skies are gray, she tries
to make him happy, things
just turn out that way.

She'll never know
how much he loves her
and yet he loves her so much
he might lay down his old guitar
and walk her home, musician
singing with the voice alone.

Oh love is sweet and love is all, it's
evening and the purple shadows fall
about the baby and the toddler
on the bed. It's true he loves her
but he should have told her,
he should have, should have said.

Foolish evening, boy with a foolish head.
He sighs like a flower above his instrument
and his sticky fingers stick. He fumbles
a simple chord progression,
then stares at the neck.
He never seems to learn his lesson.

Here comes the rain. Oh if she were only
sweet sixteen and running from the room again,
and if he were a blackbird
he would whistle and sing
and he'd something
something something something.

COLLOQUIAL EUROPE

Mr Sharp gets out of the taxi.
He doesn't smoke but lights his pipe.
His various friends walk up and down.
'And this? What do you call this?' says the driver.
'In the land I come from,' says Mr Sharp,
'it is called a taxi.' Then he waits on the quiet platform.

'Good seats but a bad train. Don't you think?'
Someone is speaking. 'And that trunk beside you,
is it heavy?' 'Heavy? Why, yes,
it is heavy, inside it I have the whole
city of Budapest.' 'Ah Budapest! always
so beautiful; myself I am travelling west.'

And it's so strange to stroll from the train
straight into the capital. There are not many houses
in the little street, just a boy eating a crayon.
He has visited his uncle, a village far in the hills,
traversing the woods beyond the stormy river.
Now he is home. He opens the door and explains.

You see a courtyard beyond the courtyard
and remember the work of a well-known artist:
a scatter of clouds in the sky, and sunlight
on the fine new library – 'one that will surely hold
all of our books.' And beyond there are pinewoods,
included, of course, to make the picture perfect.

'A few leaves, a few clouds, and
the fat doctor was halfway up the stairs.'
How my heart sank when I saw him!
But he behaved magnificently, unlike

I must say, my publisher, who is pleasant enough
but won't even glance at my poetry.

Now here is my coffee, just as I like it.
The town is still whole, and very interesting,
and my leg is well again, thank you,
after my recent trip to Australia. The mist
will be gone by the weekend. We shall sing
and stroll in the surroundings

for Autumn is always pretty in these parts,
black smoke on the trunks,
old towns with towers and medieval houses,
and then there is always the Spring:
I like to wait for my late lady friend
whenever the ice on the Danube is breaking.

He carries the lady's fur on his arm.
He has already waited for seventeen minutes,
eyeing the five or six plain girls who are also waiting.
So sad that this is only a Hungarian lesson.
But my dear fellow, it goes without saying.
It goes without saying.

Well, he sent her a postcard but, the fool,
he should have known she wanted a letter!
On what trivialities it depends, whether one takes a wife.
I suppose I should write all this down.
Now let us stroll with our valuables,
as no one here is inclined to be punctual.

'He was always speaking of the Great Powers,
my thoughtful young friend; so much of a hurry.
Why he almost . . .' But look, the porter

holds out his empty hand. 'What,
please, is this?' 'Ah, in New Zealand,'
says Mr Sharp, 'we call that the tip. Taxi!'

Hence the pale, hopeless voice of the waiter,
who knows that my soup tastes like a ticket
for a magnificent cruise on the Danube.
Ah my love, on the coast of the past
and desiring to make your acquaintance,
tell me, where shall we dine tonight?

But now I prefer my Hungarian lesson,
so we want none at all of this music.
'The hotel is nice with rather small rooms
and we left a few coins on the table;
then the waiter came and took the cutlery, yes,
while the bread it remained in the basket.'

And see, our friends, smiling and chatting,
have already left the garden. They argue
whether the Chain Bridge is older,
and therefore a little more beautiful. Why?
Curd tart or poppy noodles? Of course you do.
Goodbye, goodbye, goodbye . . .

'A tranquil place, but I really preferred it
in Linz.' Her impertinent nose
which I glimpsed through the powder.
And now this wonderful night at the theatre.
We sit in the clumsy audience,
and kiss a great deal as the great curtain rises.

PETAL

A metal road right through
the new National Park
and we pulled up on the verge
to check for damage. Someone

up in a tree. No, but blink
and it's true, someone up in a tree
waving at you. 'Hello there,
did life get that boring

to make you climb, are you
up there all of the time
or what? Well one of our tyres
is totally shot, we hit these flowers

you see, and managed to hang on
for the best part of an hour
and even believed we were heading
safely for home when the car started

veering towards the edge
and of course that
drop on the left had us worried,
so, well, you know . . .' No answer,

just a high shadow in twilight
at the edge of a sidetrack
quietly watching us scrape
flowers from the headlights.

MAGPIE CROONING

Cold like the cold southern ocean,
and cold like the flatterer's stone,
she shivers and shifts and lifts her gaze
to the bird's mixed-up view of the morning.
Stewart Island, we call this place,
where we plan to go one day, bush
and a crescent of sand, a memory,
some sort of memory of a face,
and the woman listens for a moment or two
then calls the children in to dinner.
They sit at the table while she swims
in silence at the bottom of a wave.
'If you see this woman, you will go to heaven.
If you see her children, you will travel.
If you smile in English, they will sing.'
But no one does anything,
only the macrocarpa with its lonely shuffle,
making at least a hundred yards along the coast
– almost lost, but you bring a mind
to the mystery of things like this
and sing a song to make the branches miss you,
making a shadow flap towards your hand.
Sheet music! Light of a star,
light of the moon, shells of their brightness.
You walk on the shore and see the children,
single son, single daughter,
and you glimpse her at midnight
and you don't know what to say.
So cold and you don't know what to say.
(You join the orchestra and sail away,
blue postcard on the water.)

AN AMERICAN MARRIAGE

He forced her into the forced
which was the forest in America.
How dark it was there – and disappointing
under the branches, though no relief,
given he only wanted to talk to her.

Sing something, he said. He sat and waited,
and she bit her wrist till the blood came.
Nothing doing, no song in the darkness:
she watched him approaching, love
in his pocket. But sky? But sky up there?

Sing something, she said, and he made these
bubbles of sound. In another life he had been
a king or a conjuror, just going around
and around in these circles: court circle,
magic circle, the ring he would slip on her finger.

IN THE STUDIO

She really was drawing! And it was
good, she had never quite realised.
She had brought out his fine
determined chin, a hint of brains.

'I think it's absolutely . . .' he said,
'but surely you can learn to do sunshine,
can't you?' But of course she can't.
It's a long, long sitting today,

gray light and makeshift easel, clouds,
and as he finishes speaking
she steps back from the undeniable likeness:
kind eyes, the strong familar jaw, ugh,

you look like that. They woke the next day,
the sea outside was choppy, she cooked
the breakfast but she might be ill.
'Look at yourself as you are, no one

could call it pleasant.' The big forehead,
those eyes and their steady dilation,
beginning again and again
whenever she says she is finished.

BETWEEN THE COUGH AND THE HOWL

Between the cough and the howl
hunger goes missing. It was in the oven,
then on the table, then nowhere at all.
Oh, I'm sorry, a friend just came in.

Yes, a friend came into the room and smiles.
He smiled and shows his terrific teeth.
Just kidding, he says, a wee surprise . . .
And indeed he was smiling already.

THE GREAT FIRE OF TORONTO

First I would like the alarm,
the elevators ringing, all systems
complete on our property.

But the problem of all possible areas!
I apologise and the system continues,
and now I would like alarms.

Thus the fire works, and elevators go,
moving the morning; emergency
teams admire the dawn.

You can return to your rooms now,
making your stay a pleasant one.
Here is a newspaper, here is normal

operations. And here is the fire chief,
his men and his flames,
waving his terrible minutes.

RED DREAM

She was a chaste girl
when she picked herself a husband;
then the old man swallowed gold and died

so she decided to be a poet.
Or maybe she told him beforehand,
sad phrases there at the bedside.

A sigh came from each branch in the garden.

★

On Monday, a dozen rhyming couplets,
on Tuesday the beauty of peach blossom.
And the next day she went to the funeral.

★

By the weekend she had crossed everything out,
garden and flute and each of the household servants.
The words were all terrible.

★

Yet near the end of the song
she could hear the singer approaching,
a hesitant step in the garden,

and she felt her heart lift with her pen.
Willow gate, oh willow willow . . .
It was time to start again.

THE MISSING CHILDREN

There is a story that tells
where the children slept,
a map that marks all of the places.
And there is a song one wrote
that tells how they felt.
It even shows some of them sleeping.

These are the pines
we saw when we woke,
those who woke. This is snow;
and these are the clouds
above pine, reminding of home.

So many years ago!

And already I see the maps
spread out on the floor –
the mothers and fathers,
the uncles and aunts, all
kneeling on carpet, their heads
meeting over the forest.

OPOUTERE NEST SONG

Sky and water, quiet
sand. Little whistle
that gets up and goes.

BLADE & SWING

A boy getting pleasure
from holding a razor,
the glimpse of a life to come

where he foams and watches
himself grow wise in the mirror,
that is one thing. But

I do not know whether
the boy I imagine
is a real boy

or is me or my father
or even my son.
I suppose it must

at least be one
of us three, trying to forget
the facts of his life

in whatever he can't forget,
and still finds hard to see.
Now memory (a sudden breath)

lifts me on to the swing, and I swing
by myself, sensing behind me
someone who is happy

(like me), a bit pushed for time,
or pushed beyond time
someone still pushing

who used to be pushing.

AIN FOLKS

On the road between Aye and Och Aye
the days I was searching
for word of my ancestors

I heard a bit of a song beginning
over by the side of the road. It was
my grandfather somewhere

beyond the railway line
calling and waving, coming to say
he won't buy me a bicycle.

No, he says, no; and then writes
it in a letter – after which I suppose
there's something about the weather.

★

Well I never knew him anyway,
first boy with a bike in all Derry
says my mother, who also tells

how he ran off with the blacksmith's daughter,
a girl who went to her own wedding
but never to one of her children's

★

certainly not to my mother's,
who took her Chemistry degree
to a hotel bar about an inch

above Antarctica, while he kept on riding
to his signal box out on the line
between Edinburgh and Kings Cross,

keeping his eye on the time,
the pure slog of rails up the incline,
the two making their way together

*

till they pause at the level crossing there
and he quietly switches the points
from yon bonnie banks

to the likewise purple heather.

THE ENGLISH TEACHER

My mother was teaching Polish soldiers.
Each day at four o'clock they marched down to the school.
This was in Scotland, Prestonpans, near Edinburgh.
'Salt pans,' says my mother, 'the monks
would make salt in the pans.'

They needed the language for the invasion of Europe;
also they wanted to meet people.
Everyone likes to get along socially.

There was a dashing sergeant.
He had only the one word of English.
At the end of each class, he clicked his heels,
opened a silver case and said, 'Cigarette?'

But my mother didn't smoke.
She stood at the blackboard, cleaning off phrases.

'Just words,' she says, 'only expressions.'
I am a soldier. I am your friend.
My mother was in her late twenties.
'I didn't know your Dad then.'

He was in San Francisco
in a nightclub called 'The Lion's Den',
or he was waking at dawn in the State of Nevada
on a train crossing America . . .

while among the Poles there was one,
a sad man who stood out from the bunch;
the Russians had locked him away,
back when they were still helping Hitler.

He had been a carpenter.
But his wife and children,
they might be dead, might be anywhere,
he might never know where they were.

The long trains laboured south
with their troops and ammunition:
two engines in front, and one at the back.

The soldier made a wooden plaque
and left it with my mother;
also a thank you letter . . .

'Give me more detail,' I say.
'You know, to put in the poem.'

But what happened to the plaque,
my mother can't remember.
'It was lovely,' she says.
All she recalls is the carpenter's sadness.

The letter she carried all the way to New Zealand,
till somewhere in the South Island,
shifting from place to place,
packing or unpacking, somehow she lost it.

Someone had written it out for him,
maybe one of the officers.
Yours faithfully, it said, or yours sincerely,
and every last word was set down correctly.

DOCTOR ZHIVAGO

The big stage and golden curtain,
stars high up in the ceiling, one of
the few films I think he would have seen.

The sound of violins, then darkness
about the wide, white screen. I can hear
the sound of my father coughing.

THE PRAIRIE POET

All day shovelling small snow,
and look, western light
at my window.

AN AMAZING WEEK IN NEW ZEALAND

So for six days he crusaded
and on the seventh he flew to Australia

Athletic Park, April 1959:
a southerly straight off Cook Strait,
the microphone bandaged in gauze.

Here in Balclutha there is quiet sunshine
and we sit on the grass,
waiting for the voice over the landline.

Our togs are back on the bus.
We have been promised
a swim afterwards.

Come forward. You come.

★

Thus in the capital
the Christ folk watch and pray,
they have bibles and binoculars

and they shake their hymn sheets
in goodly company
while we sit still and listen only

Come, you come

to the tall undeniably handsome man
(who is forty but looks thirty)

with an easy, friendly manner
and a sound–system
flown in from Melbourne.

His face goes by on the tram.

★

His face goes by on the bus
Lord Lord yes
past shops with unrepeatable prices

but I am not
going forward. I am sitting
here on the grass

constructing my hut in the pines,
planks with a sway,
high life on a windy day.

I am sitting here on the grass
watching the old wolf,
Akela, finger his hip-flask

★

and I smile. A scout smiles and whistles
under all difficulty. Wicked Shere Khan!
Stupid Bandar-log! I am pure as the rustling wind.

But how to read Nature's secrets . . .
The feathers and fur on the ground,
a rabbit lying there like a glove . . .

What is it evidence of?

*

I'm going to ask you to do something hard and tough. I'm going to ask you to get up out of your seat, hundreds of you, get up out of your seat, and come out on this field and stand here quietly, reverently. God has spoken to you. You get up and come. I can hear you in your heart. You want a new life. You want to live clean and wholesome for Christ. The Lord has spoken to you . . .

*

But I want to remember
the three hundred things
a bright boy can do . . .

the boy as this or that,
chorister or scientist,
the boy as magician

sweet talking

the girl doomed to cremation
and the cries of spectators
who see flames and smoke

then bones and a skull, then there's
only their own applause

*

for everyone's safe of course
and the boy's busy investigating
more astonishing

things: invisible ink
and a musical ring,
a puzzling and wonderful chicken,

while Christ comes again and again
in the clouds, cumulo
nimbus, the wind and the rain, riding

those parallel lines that end
in a point, in a friendly warning:

'Dear King Prempel. You must give up
human sacrifice and slave-trading.'

★

Lift your eyes from the page.

God's glance is a wind
that goes through you,
mysterious language

that teaches a scout to see sign
in a tangle of stars
or a twig or two

while lipstick on your collar
(your first record)

tells its tale on you, black
with that yellow label

and you follow the narrow trail
through falling leaves,
sign after sign leading

to where the ground is level
at the foot of the cross,
and there is Billy on his knees . . .

You see Billy Graham up here.
But he is not the main actor.
The main actor is the one who comes to hear.

And look! the pickpocket returns the wallet
and Billy gets to his feet,
surprised but friendly.

He has the vigour of three men.
He shakes your hand before he strikes.

A smile and a nod.
A smile and a nod.
He's giving the glory to God.

★

The boom of bronze over the landline.
The West Coast farmer stops milking his cows.
A boy stops making strange noises.

But how do you 'get right' with God?
What is soteriology? All I know is
people are changing their lives today.

We're ending the old life of sin.

★

That's it . . . that's it . . .
come on . . . there are others coming . . .

Just as I am, without one plea
But that Thy blood was shed for me

sing it again softly as others come . . .
say that eternal Yes to the Lord.

★

And Fay the Widgie . . . How is she?
Bright lipstick! My word!

All brazen façade and crazy parties,
leopard skin pants and a pony tail.

But now her parents are puzzled.
Where is their self-centred daughter?
She hasn't gone to town.

Come on. You come down.

★

The publican wants God as a partner,
the businessman, the wife, oh
the girl with scars on her wrists
taking her baby to God

the shiftless drunk no one trusts
who lives in a packing shed
the days are weeks and the weeks are months

Doreen and Fay and Don the borstal-boy

and God is not a clean shirt but a clean body
lifting from the pool
after a width underwater, the dazzle
of water pouring back. So

that after you stop saying No to God
you feel one hundred per cent.
You know you're
in trouble: you know
you need help
from the tender-hearted Lord.

*

The boy as ventriloquist –
the distance and resonance
of approaching noise: man

in the chimney talks
to the man in the roof, both puzzled
by those muffled cries

from the cellar. Then you make a mistake,
then make the effort to make
crowd-pleasing music,

the *pangka-bongka* of the banjo
the *zhing-sching* of the cymbals
the *plim-blim* of the harp

steady *beat* of the heart

or the Jew's-harp: *whanga-
whonga whee-whaw
whoodle-onga eedle-ongle*

whow-zeedle oodle-ee whay-
whonga whaw: almost impossible
to do, like the roar

of an excited crowd, the sound
of winter skaters, a choir singing
as the folk go forward, one

by one, *now come, you come* . . .

★

One thousand miles of miracle
lead to where the ground is level
at the foot of the cross

and here we are on our knees
inspecting the world of loss:
broken twigs, a hair,

a scrap of food,
big sign and small sign, let
nothing escape you,

trampled grass, a drop of blood,
a button, a match, a leaf,
thing like a glove . . .

But God is not here,
not in sunshine, not
in God's open air

but somewhere altogether elsewhere

in dark accumulations
in winter macrocarpa

★

in the needle of sound in a circle
Lipstick on your collar

the nervous current of the tiger's claw
the windy cry from the pack

★

Akela! Akela!

★

who takes another swig
then sucks on his Life Saver

whow-zeedle oodle-ee
whay-whonga
whaw . . . Lord

Lord, I am
not going forward.

MOONLIGHT

Kate Gray (1975–1991)

I start up a conversation
with occasional Kate. Too late,
too late, but with a big sigh
she appears in the sky.

I tell her the home doesn't forget –
her mother's lullaby step
still reaches the chair
where her father sits deep in the forest.

I hear myself saying
please and please and please;
I want to go back
to the start of the nineties.

Sleepless night, big almond eyes,
and a hand rocks a pram in the passage;
from somewhere a long way
outside of our houses

the moon sends its light to this page.

WHAT TO CALL
YOUR CHILD

LANDSCAPE WITH BRIDE

Song of the flute, the river's
armoured bed: gray weather,
blue weather. 'Can't you tell

I'm asleep?' she said. But could he ever
begin to turn it down? The river? So the notes
hovered above her pillow-cradled head,

they were like footprints in snow,
he thought, which was like her gown,
and they ended at a tree which was bare,

which was empty, which was probably
when he ought to have turned to go;
plus there was moonlight,

then the long climb in moonlight,
the trunk up above growing longer and longer,
still grooming its bachelor shadow.

PICNIC AT WOODHAUGH

Dunedin: 1863

In the half light of the Early Settlers Museum
there is a world of trees; they rise
on their roots to steal the sun.

But there is no sun.

A small bridge negotiates the stream:
a log and rail, with steps at either end,
a stile across a fence of water.

★

Men and women
in a Dunedin clearing
detailed off

behind a long white cloth
where four plates and half-a-dozen bottles
represent the feast.

Dark nineteenth-century light
but enough still there to show us
where the light has been . . .

Each figure has a face, a small one,
and they all face out. They
seem to have finished eating.

★

Fifty good folk at a picnic –
the men mostly standing, the ladies afloat
on the grass with their children –

plus two who have come to the front:
a woman dressed as a man, black trousers,
and, perched on her lap, a fellow in tails.

They are performers, perhaps?
Or even the most important guests?

They stare straight out like all the rest.

★

The exhibition catalogue says
that 'looming verdure threatens
to engulf the group'.

And it is true: they are tiny
and trite among the trees:
safely ashore, yet still at sea.

★

They know how to stand
on the deck of a ship approaching land . . .

★

There are strollers elsewhere in the park,
some lost in a world of shade,
fading or about to fade

*

two of whom manage to be clear –
latecomers, they cross the bridge
and aim for the middle of the canvas,

pausing only to admire the first recorded
Dunedin dog: a trunk on legs, eyes on a snout,
elephant ears, tail sticking out

*

though in fact the dog is walking with them

*

and the man looks faintly embarrassed,
as if stepping across
the surface of a trampoline.

*

His knees are too near the ground,
and he compensates with a puzzled forward lean:
the incline, perhaps, of thoughtful conversation,

or of someone planning to found a nation

*

while she . . .

*

but really, she can hardly hear . . .
What was that he said?

*

And it is so *very* hard to see –
and so she takes his arm and advances

holding aloft her *parasol*

*

which like her, she thinks, is pretty but unexpected

a fresh flower of the forest,
a wee bit smaller than her head.

AMERICA

In this way we came to the place of sacrifice.
There were savages, several of the gods of whom they speak,
plus friends I hadn't seen in years.
Harry and Iris were the first of 'our crowd'

to marry. And here they were amazingly
still together, two kids in tow, just waiting.
Iris had tiny pictures tattooed on her lids,
and one day I promise to tell you

exactly what they were, but for the moment at least
will simply say the one word, *technicolor*.
I asked Iris after her pleasant mother, whom I thought
I remembered. She wept, and held her head.

'The body was never returnèd.' It sounded
somewhat desperate, that extra syllable. Still
she sat at my invitation on my knee,
a forty-two-year-old, uncertain woman,

while Harry took the kids and his old look of alarm
off to an adjoining clearing. Year in year out
the place grew more complete, while they lingered
just out of earshot, just along the street, and all this time

I gazed into Iris's eyes, trying to recall the one more thing
I had wanted to ask – or even at last to tell her.
But now, alas, there would be no telling: she was asleep
between the god's blue eye and his high blue mountain.

WHAT TO CALL YOUR CHILD

Veronica's heart belongs to her
and not to Troy. Thus the boy
lives in slow disaster, by smoke
and scattered sand; he stands in the gray water
or stalks the shore,
and when Veronica's heart
is washed up there, he doesn't love her
any more. Thus guitar joins guitar
and she is there at last in the ocean
but now he doesn't want to kiss her;
in fact he hates his sister. Oh she is herb,
she is skin, Christ in his skeleton,
the whole of the world he wants,
maybe jasmine. She knows the quietest name
of the wind, and says it but he cannot hear.
He makes a bird of paper (bird of timber,
bird of trees) and throws it to the breeze.
He places his foot inside his father's shoe
and listens to his mother talking:
'Grace has come back and Olive will be, too.'

LONESOME

I was so lonesome
and as usual
I could cry.

I went out of the house.
No single star
was itself –

just mountain and sky
making the old
horizon high . . .

and behind me
he tiptoed in
through the door.

Was he really so desperate?
So poor? Years later
I imagine him

pointing the remote
at the screen he's grown tired of
and recalling

his one lucky moment:
a man walking
away, and the suddenly

shining interior: the irrelevant
dirty floor – and the key
lifting its clumsy

light to the lock
and lodging there
deep in the cylinder.

AUBADE

His heart still bled.
So he woke within a ballad.

'Come soon, if that is what you meant.
I am lonely,
I am rough and insufficient.'

Oh he was certainly pale
and later he was pallid.

And oh his poor heart bled.

Verse or refrain?
There was a single willow
and then the wind from Spain.

Yet what came first
and what was after?

All he remembered was he left her
by a stream or tree, or underneath a star,
he left her beside her laughter.

INESILLA

I am here, Inesilla,
gazing up at your window.
All of Seville
is darkness and sleep.

I am here with my cloak,
and my guitar and sword,
with what makes me bold.
I am here at your window.

Do you sleep, Inesilla? Well
I will soon wake you with song,
and if the old fellow stirs
there's always this blade.

Ah let fall from the sill
that handhold of silk.
Why are you so slow?
Can it mean there's a rival?

I am here, Inesilla.
I am here at your window.
All of Seville
is darkness and sleep.

THE ALBUM

What can you gain from my name?
It will die – like the sad scrawl
of a wave on a far-off shore,
like night as it sighs in the woods.

On the pale, remembering page
there'll be only a trace,
marks on a headstone
in some strange, untranslatable tongue.

For what can remain? Lost
in the years and the tempests of feeling,
my name cannot last in your life
like some delicate keepsake.

Yet on a day of despair, in a small space
of calm, say it aloud out of your sadness; say
'Somewhere I may still be remembered;
there's a heart in the world, where I live.'

GRAPES

after Pushkin, and for John Buck

But who can feel sadness
for the roses? The spring
goes, and they fade

just as the grapes I love
begin to ripen on the vine,
climbing across

the slopes above the house,
day after day
until at last they stand

in all the valleys and the golds
of autumn . . . where now
they are long and slender

and the light shines through them
as through the fingers
of a young girl's hand . . .

PETENERA

The dark lift of the lungs,
the lungs of the high, exhausted dancer
who does his sprawled, exhausted dance
while outside snow cancels the big

uncomfortable universe. How far down the floor is
where the guitar has been abandoned,
as in a young man's stumbling poem,
among cigarette ends and betting slips,

where we find also an ancient powder compact
belonging to the singer's mother,
plus a few coins, now of no consequence,
sitting quietly on their shadows.

VALEDICTORY

Thank you for listening so patiently
to the poems that once made me famous.
I expect I rather run on. Now, let me turn
to and fro through the pages. Ah . . .

well, yes. And thank you for staying to hear
the one which might make me rich.
In a moment I will read it
and then after that we will be finished,

though poems, as I think you may know,
can go on and on lasting the distance, and sometimes
the reader will take them to heart, and thus
one's words grow a mite more accomplished,

clearer, yet . . . ah . . . far more mysterious,
like some last shot at happiness;
so that when, after the last somewhat desperate kiss,
you look up from the page,

well, the main thing surely you see is –
ah, here we are –
not the executioner's face
but his arms covered in bruises.

DOMESTIC

She threw him the tea-towel.
Get yourself on the end of that.
What a strange woman!
Her novel had flowers in it,
a horse called Thunder,
but it never really sold.
Maybe not enough reviews,
maybe the wrong reviewers . . .
Strange woman, out in the kitchen,
chopping onions and dropping
bits down her butterfly front
as she wept and wept
and sustained it – thoroughly
losing the plot. So that was the end
. . . of what? . . . of *that*, if not
of the next little spell.
She came back through
and threw him the tea-towel.

LAST DAYS OF THE DOGE

I sat back in the gondola
while the doctors moved towards me.
A view of the snow, the dog
wagging its tail: phlegmatic,

automatic, just like that.
I sat back in the gondola
and called hello. Two
pretty girls smiled and pressed on.

They paused on the bridge, staring back,
probably wanted to hear my song.

I sat back in the gondola and called hello.
I sat back in the gondola,
hearing the mastiff whine
and watched as the doctors moved towards me.

And now even the girls had gone,
pretty much forever,
and I was there on the black water
in the left-over, sinister weather.

So at least it was time.
Sing gondolier! I cried
and as we sang
we sank together.

COLIN

McCahon said jump
and now we all

jump, sort of,
sometimes, anyway

look, it's hard
to lift

when you haven't
got the energy

nor the musculature
nor the gift,

it takes a pack
of courage

to shift
the Mustang in the drive

the one with
the painting in it

with the man
jumping over onions

each onion a file
of fine lines

across the face
of the man

who stares at the canvas
and really can't resist

*

and the further the eyes
jump, Colin

told me, the firmer
the feet

on the ground:
Muriwai, 1969

(big tidal sound)

we felt shellfish rising
from beneath

our feet. We were their
sky and they

our firmament.
No one was

going by
which I think

gave Colin
much of his advantage

★

which leaves, I suppose
the Norfolk pine

3 kids calling
50 feet high

as if they could
touch the sky

as if the ocean
were their father

as if they
would rather

*

sit on
the empty

beach
write 'walk

with me'
then vanish

into the aloneness:
oh that feels

fairly
solitary all right

that feels like
the dark landscape

& the horizon
we have heard of

& the light.

In Memoriam 'Storm Warning'

LANDSCAPE WITH PINES

The light touching the concrete is the light I like, I never cared for any other. You came up the path then, you came through patches of weed and wood, dense despair that made you continue forward, a misprint or two, a simple thing to say. After a moment I looked up and saw you. You weren't walking now, it was a question of clouds, things that went wrong and took a range of shapes – not shapely things so much as systems we never cared for, things that meant nothing then continued. How many times did we talk on that path, watching the children, how many times did we walk together, hand in hand, even in our most hopeless conversations. Others came by, hand in hand or separate items or together. We liked the lonely ones, the ones who only had eyes for you, and you were walking and wailing, moving among the patches of light in that place, cloud over the simple pine we paused beside and imagined the children planting, with the headmaster watching and his wife beside him. This was how it happened in the fifties. The tree entered the earth and would grow tall. The wife would find someone else, a kinder man but still within the world of education, the clouds would float above the path. And what would we two do? I loved you then, and meant to tell you. An end to all pretence. You stood stock still and still looked lonely. Nothing could possibly matter. Thus nothing comes clear and at last, we find, the tree is deep in a forest. Children walk there; they sit on the dark needles, counting cones into a sack, occasionally calling for their parents.

BETWEEN DRINKS

Names for paint,
for carpet – the warrior
lays down his sword,

asks how you are,
then drives to Auckland
in an unmarked car.

★

All that countryside! so
nice in the books
where scenery sticks to the pages

but, you know, we found ourselves
biting our tongues
each time the caravan entered the valley.

★

'Well, as it turns out
she couldn't actually stand him . . .'

★

So maybe it was finally
time to buy the fridge and go:

Dutch White or Sand,
a wee splash
of green by the window.

NEVERTHELESS

The rose can't hurt itself.
It rips and interrupts the hand

and then when the hand
does something else

the rose says: *Praise*
the rose says: *Nourish*.

Such trust in the garden!

Big old moon
and even older moonbeams.

But eventually we all know that.

THE GONG

Hillsides brisk with beauty:
and the great gong is slung between trees.
Now William Butler Yeats hits it hard.
The sound moves out across water,
touching America, tormenting Europe –
and Ireland is weightless again.

FIST ROUND A MAGNET

Always myself though.
And now the scream
just entering the bird.

MILLENNIAL

Under an eyelash
under a stone
but no he lived
under her fingernail.
He was the silent moon.

So much foliage
crammed inside the bride!
He was the silent moon.
In Spring the husband
was dark in every language.

And so on and so on.
And soon the skeleton
was biting its way through the badlands
to where she sat on the floor
reviving her bicycle.

The song when it came
was light left in the radio;
it started up like a car
about to enter a river
and then it was over.

LUCK: A VILLANELLE
for Peter Dunkerley

After a time of drought, the whole heart dances
(You might have been a priest, and her a nun):
You turn around, and turn around to Frances.

For luck is a thing of losses, then advances;
It offers the rain and next it sends the sun.
After a waste of time, the whole heart dances.

A chemist's world is magic stuff and trances,
And a gin and tonic's good for everyone:
You turn around, and fill a glass for Frances.

So why do they take so long, these wondrous chances?
How did a Dunkerley take out Division One?
After a stumbling time, the old heart dances.

Everyone knows where Scotland is, and France is,
But geography will never get things done.
Still you spin the globe, and see it stop at Frances.

For luck always meant embracing all the chances;
And sometimes we glimpse the moon beside the sun.
After a time of drought the whole heart dances,
You turn around, and turn around to Frances.

RECOVERED NOAH

A big pile of sparkle,
teeth for the wedding.
The bride knows every attractive song.

She sits on the floor
reviving her bicycle.
But I forgot the elegant rip,
sky like a thousand miles of Jesus.

★

At last the waters settled.

★

He gazed down
at the deep, diminished trees.
And then he could hear the bird.

PLEDGE

for Christine and Andrew

Oh it is serious and it changes
like something in a play. Comes a day
the pledge lifts quietly from the page
and to utter it at all can take an age.

Nothing prepares us for the world so large.
Generations of example, tales
and photographs and words,
but no presage: it makes us simple.

There you go, past family and friends
and family and friends –
a procession in the street –
along the ordinary, crowded passage

and into the *paysage*.

A FINAL SECRET

Every morning, we the Loop say:
'Will you enter creation?
I will enter creation.'
Then we have breakfast.

It is better if one Loop asks the question
and the next Loop answers,
and thus around the room,
especially if there are many Loop present,
until you are done. But if you are alone,
you may question yourself
and make your answer in a somewhat different voice.

Or you can use the same one, it is entirely your choice.
We the Loop do not make love any more,
we do not make decisions,
but we travel and explore, loving unlikely distance.
We have been called a nomadic nation.
We are always getting into our stride.

Today we crossed the sea of Dunedin, the great
     pedestrian waters.
We elbowed so many people aside.
We were in haste. We had heard
of another branch of the Loop, perhaps a tribe,
or perhaps it was only a village,

and, as fully expected, we woke on another shore.
The sun was shining on the wet sand, on the sails,
and somewhere ahead lay the heart of the nation.
Will you enter creation?
I will enter creation.

ANTARCTIC FIELD NOTES

for Nigel Brown & Chris Orsman

HOOSH

I
Highest, driest, coldest, windiest
continent, doubling its size in winter:
Emily's gone to Antarctica.

All that red hair on the ice!

★

Blue eyes, summer deep field
at Granite Harbour, an orange tent
between Asgard and Olympus

while I stand in the library, lost
between Acquisitions and Closed Reserve
and try to look after her

★

into the endless November light
where the mist
touches Discovery, touches

Terror, and the glaciers calve and thunder,
melt-water of whatever was freezing here
a million years before Christ

★

or I take the ten-minute trip
from the middle of town
to visit Antarctica's secrets

at my own pace. Great God! this
is an awful place. Ah look
how they're doing it by the book

⋆

reading the labels of tins,
Boiled Beef, Le lait condensé
to pass the time of day:

darts, cards, dominoes, and chess;
Amundsen plays the *Apache Waltz*
while Scott stares at the Christmas tree

⋆

and Emily's drill goes down

⋆

and over the water, fluttering
through snow, comes
the sound of *The Mikado*.

II
Whiteout. A cairn in a sea of sastrugi.
The blizzard repeats itself
every twelve minutes

though it is mostly silence
making your ears ring,
making you move along whenever

you hear the tin dogs yelping

*

while Mawson ties
the soles of his feet
back on

*

and we
hop on the Snowmaster,

riding through darkness
and the wind and song
to Butter Point, Cape Chocolate,

back to the world of questions
and the welcome home – the voice,
the hand-grip . . . it chokes me,

it cannot be uttered.

III
'It is only sleep in the cold,'
the son tells his mother.
It is only the open air.

But we are strolling indoors
in a world where
it's even better than being there.

In a room made entirely of ice
Oscar Wisting sits at his sewing machine,
stitching tent after tent,

dreaming of whortleberry jam

＊

and at the end of the day
every explorer returns to his diary,
inscribing entry after entry

about the drudgery of courage,
sawing through ice, the absolute hush
I am, I am, I am

Symington's Soup
diluting the pemmican,
seal consommé on Christmas Day

＊

and always the strange desire to play:
the crystal snort of the banjo,
Griffith Taylor on a bicycle,

Byrd flying over the Pole
alone, alone, Shackleton
writing a poem,

Professor Drygalksi (1902)
taking photographs from a tethered balloon,
in touch with his ship by telephone.

IV
'Fine weather and steady sea,
and all looks hopeful and happy . . .'

except for the sun setting twice,
icebergs that fly,
the Virgin Mary standing beside

a dead man on an ice floe,
eyes with that
comfortable blue look of hope,

whatever is real beyond

*

shovels and picks and rope,
men pulling their weight,
type in the tray, everything sinking

away, dogs and men
and even endurance . . .
Fram, Terra Nova, Pourquoi-Pas;

ah surely the ship
will come to rescue us;
if only we can learn the names of ships,

somehow survive
the seventy-five
varieties of ice, lenticular

skies and katabatic winds,
all the words
lost in the archive.

v
Then we dreamed we were in Spain,
discussing the Irish question,
our heads hurting again.

For only action is tolerable,
even turning away
to harness up the dogs

we do not leave our vehicle,
we do not move in darkness
or in mist. *Make lists,*

make lists, question but
do not question the treacherous
lid of each crevasse

★

whenever you ride in tourist weather,
in whiteout and blizzard, whenever
the clouds ride high

above the fossil record,
whenever you cruise into the polar cavern
descending below the icy ocean

★

25 million tons of krill

★

into bad light
and doubtful light and absent light,
just sitting tight until at last

the sun rises and we see
men get their shadows back,
crawling below the blast

or climbing to the crow's-nest
to find nothing in sight,
no savages nor bears,

no one to mention Heaven to,
only rough notes which tell a tale
which we read as we eat our hairy stew

★

hoosh

★

pony mixed with penguin
mixed with whale, seal
rissoles and the stewed paws

of huskies, a wonderful
banquet on deck,
ice-blink and water-sky,

and we woke from our dream of food
to find the food
sliding towards the water,

a pod of nodding orca, the pack
breaking and breaking
and taking us with it . . .

VI
Geology! the helicopter rises,
the scientists crowd around,
and Emily's drill goes down

through a thousand years of ice:
ghost of a dog, ghost of a pony,
Oates going deeper and deeper

below the surface

★

still perfectly himself,
still gone for some time,
lost in whatever Emily might find

of sediment and algae,
the movement and retreat
of seasons, time passing

in samples and traces
– *beech and conifer* –
stuff from the core

to take home and question
and even then perhaps
not quite be sure . . .

★

May the years of her life
look after her.
Emily's gone to Antarctica.

INTO THE ICE SHELF

Right ten degrees rudder!

Right ten degrees rudder, aye!
My rudder is right ten degrees.

Very well.
Ease your rudder.

Ease my rudder, aye.

Very well.
Shift your rudder. Rudder amidships.

Rudder amidships, aye.
My rudder is amidships.

Homelight. Quiet light.

Very well. Steady as she goes.

★

On the bridge
the captain's wearing
his red *Polar Sta*r baseball cap.

Weddell seals, orcas,
a single minke . . .

(but I've missed it)

& there's the *Marco Polo*.

*

Setting course one four nine.
Checking zero two two.

Very well.

Rudder amidships.

Rudder amidships, aye.
Rudder is amidships.

Very well.

Horizon.

BLOOD FALLS

Rusty glacier snout:
a scatter of canvas
between ice and stone

and in the morning
he hears a stream
running beneath the ice.

*

Here he is with his cautious life.

*

Cold music: he breaks
the delicate pane
and sprawls face down

to drink the unnamed water;
the lake chatters like a dolphin,
like a sudden outboard motor.

SOME FRAMES

Antarctica!
where a single
footprint lasts
a thousand years

and here we are
with our
thousand footsteps
etcetera

★

or here I am
with my cautious life

sandstone and dolerite

in the pure environment
admiring the granite protocols
and colour-coded receptacles,

from time to time
cleaning my teeth
into the gray water barrel

★

while a man from Aberystwyth
takes a chainsaw to the ice.

The sun's slowly circling him.

He's doing it for Angie,
he's doing it for science.

★

Or here is a tent in Antarctica
and outside by a frozen lake
a man is smoking
a big handrolled Havana cigar

★

or

★

midnight, daylight, orange funnel

★

fumbling through many
layers he finds

his own warm cock.

TIME LAPSE

Mike returns from filming the wind
Jeanie cradles her husky.

★

On the field phone
Tim's listening in
then listening out.

★

We'll see, says someone.
But the horizon's gone.

CURRENT

And again I stand by Bryn's
twenty-thousand-dollar
Total Station

barely able
to overcome
my cold elation.

For Bryn was measuring every agitation.

And we were all of us
watching Brian suspended
from the lip of the Taylor

blue above palisades of height,
ledge after ledge of light,
columns and spills and organ pipes,

where he would shift on his rope
then steady, then spin
and hammer

the tiny yellow pegs in.

*

Yet even crossing the lake
we were walking on air,
walking on water.

Beyond the moat
lay low chapels of ice:

and each place, each palace,
did chime and tremble as we passed.

SONG

For the first time in a long time
there is sun making sunshine,
the heart sings which was once sighing,
for the first time in a long time.

Now the world is the world without trying:
the line releases the next line
and the next line, the next line –
for the first time, for the first time,

for the first time in a long time.

BLUE FLOWER

The little primus is off,
the generator's off,
the wind has dropped.

As we wait in the silence
of promise after promise
one wants to hear

the clatter of the helicopter
and another
the frozen sound of bells.

ERRATIC

Every stone a traveller:
one more darkness,
another gust of light.

GOODBYE

But my little Iroquois is shy.
She rises above the valley
and now above the wind

while far below
the scholar hands on his glacier
– moat and selvage and spine –

to yet another scholar,
who already has
the next recipient in mind.

DEEP FIELD SONG

Patch me out to Lake Bonney,
Patch me out to the ice:
Where the glaciers pour
And suspend at your door
And the world doesn't look at you twice.

And patch me out to McMurdo,
To Evans and Royds and Bird,
Where Shackleton and Scott,
By Jove, did a lot,
While admiring the tabular bergs.

But then patch me right back to Lake Bonney,
Patch me whatever the price:
The ice on the lake
Doesn't hurry or wait,
And it might be Paradise.

CAPE ROYDS

The helicopter delivers us down,
then clatters away
with its fluffy dice.

The shadowed edge
of an iceberg goes by;

I look at it twice

★

part of the view from below the tent
which is water and snow,
spurs of volcanic black,

scruffy slopes
and nuggety rises
which seem to make up a landscape

with the surprise of a lake
and a house beside the lake.

ADÉLIE

In the distance, the rookery's
tucked under the headland,
deep centuries of guano,

so that they stand in their own
pastel light, the penguins
('geese and goslings,' said Pigafetta),

on pebbles, on ancestral bones,
and continue to chatter
as I recite to them for the camera:

snow, paper, a little
shiver of language
lifting at last from the page.

FOOD CHAIN

The big chicks chase any adult
who might be a parent.

A bird waddles back from the water,
belly crammed with krill,
then drops and toboggans,
tired after all that travel,

and pauses just
at the edge of the nursery

★

where at once it's surrounded

★

while the skuas go on cruising the colony:
dangerous wings
slicing in from the edge

★

and out at sea (shouts someone)
a leopard seal has taken a penguin . . .

★

For a while, we watch the seal
play with the life it will eat;
for a while, it seizes with teeth,
then tosses the bird somewhere behind;

then turns and seizes again
and tosses it to and fro, to and fro . . .
to and fro for a bit . . .

★

and for a while Mike goes into close-up
at the edge of the cliff, filming it.

THE HUT

Four doormats domesticate you
as you enter: step by step
you leave the ice behind.

And inside, there's Edwardian order:
furniture and food,
a late-twentieth-century broom,

and now a poet sweeping the floor.

★

Minced collops, rump steak,
cans & cans of cod roe;
stewed kidneys, Roast Veal,
Flaked Tapioca, anchovies,
pickled onions; not to mention

the A1 Mulligatawny Soup
(Specially Prepared for Invalids)
1150 jars of bottled fruit,
bloater paste and Preserved Parsnip
and Moirs Mutton Cutlets

★

and outside, a mile or so
beyond the hut,
Erebus starts to go up.

FORECAST

White inside the weather,
white shadow, white shine:
low and high
white all the time.

★

Nothing patching the sky: might be
the slow bite of the beginning
or something nearing the end . . .

always the weather,
and each expedition entering weather,
always the one event of the wind . . .

THE POLAR EXPLORER'S
LOVE SONG

The goddess Hypothermia
came and held me tight
and as we kissed we drifted
in the pale, pure light.

Antarctica was in her heart
and ice lay on her breast;
she was the warmest lover
and the best.

She made the glaciers advance,
she made the ice shelf shine,
she made the skua bird take flight
above her love and mine.

DISPLAYS

Rest, preening, stretching,
yawning, scratching, shaking.

Walking, looking around,
nest building. Copulation, incubation,
withdrawn crouch.

Chase, escape, attack.
Six distinct threat displays,
involving beaks and eyes
and gape and charge.

Plus four sexual displays:
both loud and quiet mutual;
bowing; and the standard, flapping,
very frequently observed, *ecstatic*.

SCAVENGER

The skua alights among the penguins
and settles comfortably, preening.
It has just eaten a chick.
The adult birds seem not to notice it.
Death, and they seem not to notice.
It has happened now, and they do not mind.

And constantly the penguins come and go
between the land and the water.
They waddle back and forth from the rookery.
They stand once again in their guano.

But beneath the ocean, they say, it is different.
There they extend their wings
and fly far into the planet.
And when they feel they are missed
they return. They catapult up
out of the water on to the tipsy ice.

All night, which is all day, they do this.
They gather at the edge.
They go to and fro through the surface.
The astonishing leaps out of the black water continue.
The leaps into the water go on.

'LISTEN NIGEL'

Listen Nigel, I'll eat dogs if I have to;
but I sure as hell
won't eat doggerel.

★

But Nigel lies on the ground.
He's painting a hut in a blizzard,
the wide world of snow.

Actually, no, he's trapped on his canvas:
the world's painting him.

★

Meantime another skua settles like a helicopter
among the penguins.
No, really, it says, I must insist.

It wants that patch of regurgitation
which the fledgling missed.
Actually, no,

it wants the fledgling.

VISITING MR SHACKLETON

for Chris Cochran

Cool! Wow! Beautiful! Awesome!
Like going back in time.
Amazing! Historic! Finally
I am truly blessed.

Wow! History! Fantastic!
Wonderfully kept.
Shackleton's the man!
Like going back in time.

Wow! Cool! Historic! Yo!
Awesome! Privileged. Unreal!
And Thank you, God. And Happy
Birthday, Dad. And Thailand.

GOODBYE

Say goodbye to the penguins,
say goodbye to Cape Royds;
we're going down to Cape Evans
and Royds is for the boids.

EVANS

Another hut filled with food.

There's the tongue of the Barne Glacier,
a headland vanishing in storm,

and here's a shingle beach
with waves and seaweed,
drift ice nudging the shore,

and here at the edge
like just another patch of snow
is a white, wave-thrown starfish

*

wee, salty asterisk.

NOW YOU SEE IT

Mountains come close
then float away. It depends
on the weather, on the time of day,

the way the water
might go darker than everyday ink,
that darker-than-radiant blue

you used at school a lot, when you wrote
so carefully in your exercise book
the names *Oates* and *Scott*.

*

They left names but not signatures:
a crate that says *Homelight*
Rising Sun Yeast

'The Original Pad' by Croxley
a box of pure New Zealand
Creamery Butter

and all sorts of stuff
to guard against
frequent colds and coughs

(Tennyson, Browning, Tennyson)

but then the work of interpreting
would arise and interrupt
the homesick reader –

a card of safety pins
test tubes, pipettes,
a bunsen burner,

a penguin with folded flippers
quietly waiting
to be dissected

*

which reminds me that some time
before we get to the end of this

perhaps we should send
a very good wish

to the poor, puzzled
Patagonian toothfish.

GOING OUTSIDE

On the wall a tapestry

*May still your life
from day to day
harmonious flow*

and beside it a hotwater bottle
hung by the neck, spare sledge runners
propped beside a box of penguin eggs,

and just through the door
a tidy stack of seals, the blubber
still leaking after eighty years

*

and you step past them into the stables:
into ancient weather,
the dark smell of harness leather,

and there's so much hay in here,
(Nobby, Chinaman, James Pigg)
bales and bales of it, and then outside again

*

into the wind and light above the hut
where – a corpse by a kennel –
a husky's still on his chain,

and all around, the litter of heroic vision:
anchor, abandoned sledge;
boxes & broken glass & rusty nails,

courage and hope and indecision.

*

They came to interpret
or just to interrupt.
Just behind the dwelling place
Erebus starts going up.

OUTSIDE THE HUT

This pick still works.
These picks still work.

*

I could dig with those spades
and hammer in those nails.

I could look out to sea
and spy the long awaited sails.

*

Oh if he saw them he would start to sing.

*

And now he finds in the ice
the blue neck of a bottle,
cold finger ring.

ANTARCTIC STONE

in my hand
and the spine of a hill
inside the stone

dark ridge of earth & bone
then inclines and heights
and sudden drops

where whatever pours
is wind, is ice, forgetting itself
at last in light

in quiet line, horizon

THE NEXT THOUSAND

There'll be the same non-stop palaver
about who did or did not invent the pavlova.
Something like China will rise,
some sort of Empire fall –
not that we will much care, not being here at all.
Deep inside the organism there'll be the familiar orgasm.
So certainly something should happen.
Possibly arithmetic and frost
will tiptoe right to the edge of the forest;
the wild blue yonder may simply go west.

The lovetorn boy will descend
from topmast and tempest
and try to get something off his chest.
He'll stare into her eyes. Big skies.
Big skies. As for the puzzled past,
it will just get longer and longer
and generally there'll not be all that much left to squander;
though someone like Hillary
will probably climb something like Everest,
because something will probably be there.

But we won't care. Someone will work his way
up the touchline. Someone will be sighing and sighing.
Someone will soon give up trying.
Someone will make an improper suggestion.
Someone will stumble over the body in question.
Someone will want to be Moslem or Christian.
The one you love will be one in a million,
no one will visit the red pavilion;
but someone will care for the one who wept,
someone will note how the world is windswept.

There will be no more screens or screen-savers
but I believe there will still be pages.
March will give way to the furious winter's rages,
the dark night to the new day,
the schedule to the resumé. I'm sorry to say
things sometimes will and sometimes will not be
exactly what they used to be. Many words
will be thoroughly meaningless:
say goodbye to sound-byte and mini-series,
but not to miseries.

At the end of the day there'll be a pretty big ask
but not a big answer. Pines will march across
paddocks and pasture. Someone will take
someone else to task. And listen to this:
there'll be an amazing invention which might replace
    batteries.
Actually, no one will know what the fact of the matter is,
and hems will be down. Almost certainly.
The bad girl's parents will go to town.
There will be no cars but much traffic congestion.
There will still be press conferences. Next question?

Authors who stay in print will include Dickens and
    Nostradamus.
There'll be maybe a dozen more Dalai Lamas.
There'll be an amazing invention which could well
    replace pyjamas.
Someone will be out of his depth but go hell-for-leather.
Someone will be at the end of her tether.
There will be such astonishing light on the water.
The sheep will still go like lambs to the slaughter.
Some will hold back while others go racing ahead.
No one will remember our old blue shed.
Both of my children will be dead.

So goodbye to the one who knows no regrets,
who will surely be sorry; goodbye to the thundering lorry.
And goodbye to those long millennial lists,
all of the 'this and that' and 'this and this'.
And let us be glad that the big, repetitive world persists,
so safe, so dangerous . . . As for the lovers,
see how she saves him each time he rescues her,
see how they search the sky for news of weather:
such wide horizons, such amazing cloud . . .
the two coasts crushing the interior . . .

AUTHOR'S NOTE

This *Collected Poems* is made up of eight earlier books of poems: *The Elaboration, The Old Man's Example, How to Take Off Your Clothes at the Picnic, Good Looks, Zoetropes, Milky Way Bar, My Sunshine* and *What to Call Your Child*. The ordering is chronological, except that a decision to gather my Antarctic poems together under the title *Antarctic Field Notes* has meant some adjustments to the selections in the last two volumes.

The Elaboration ('Poems by Bill Manhire, Drawings by Ralph Hotere') was published in Wellington in April 1972 by Square & Circle, a new publishing venture begun by Charles Brasch and Janet Paul, and was the first in a projected series of collaborations between poets and painters. Brasch's death in 1973 meant that it was the only such title, though the first volume of a similar 'Stories and Drawings' series, O.E. Middleton's *The Loners*, had appeared in October 1972. From my point of view, the collaboration was a pretty long-distance affair, for I was living in London, and sent my share of the book to Dunedin for Ralph to work on. The publisher's format required, along with cover and drawings, a portrait of the poet by the artist, and handwritten versions of a poem each by artist and writer. (Ralph did 'The White Pebble', minus the sixth section; I did 'A Death in the Family'.) The poet had also to write a prose 'Statement'. Here is mine. It seems to me now impossibly mannered, but I'm pleased to find myself still comfortable with the sentiments.

> One asks, but never adequately answers, the question: *why write?* Meanwhile I keep noticing that the conditions of writing seem to carry less meaning than the poems which choose to give them expression. By that token, these poems are strategies for discovery, yet I am also thankful to sense that it is not their habit to articulate solutions to the business of living. They seem, more and more, to be fictions, elaborated out of the truth of this or that situation. At some point, hopefully, the elaboration ends and they come to be arbitrary facts, making their own way into the particular worlds of those people who cared to read them.

The Old Man's Example was published privately in 1990, but a note on the title verso indicates the period from which the poems date: 'This small selection of published and unpublished work comes from the two or three years when the 60s were turning into the 70s.' In fact, many of the poems – and a number of others which remain uncollected – could easily have been gathered up into *The Elaboration*, while one or two – like 'Buckets' and 'Wings' – would have been more at home in *How to Take Off Your Clothes at the Picnic*. I have added 'Sounding the Dark', which was written for Charles Brasch, founding editor of *Landfall*. (See *Landfall* 194, Spring 1997, for an account of the poem's provenance.)

How to Take Off Your Clothes at the Picnic was published in Wellington in 1977 by Don McKenzie's Wai-te-ata Press. The Wai-te-ata Press was a teaching press, then associated with Victoria University's Department of English, and all the poems in *Picnic* were handset – under Don's guidance, and by many hands. One hand turned the wind in stanza three of 'Leaving Home' into wine, and I have taken the chance to restore the original reading. There was a nice three-colour, two-page title spread, which managed to produce on the left hand opening an additional small poem: 'How to / take off / at the / picnic'. The collection was divided into three sections (section one began with 'The Incision', two with 'The Kiss', three with 'The Song'). Each section had its own epigraph and, since I think of the epigraphs as an important part of the book, here they are.

[Section one]

What does fear produce? Pallor. What does anger cause? A flush. Or what, the vice of pride? A swelling up. We refashion the statement thus: *Fear grows pale, anger flushes, pride swells*. There is greater pleasure and satisfaction for the ear when I attribute to the cause what the effect claims as its own.

Geoffrey of Vinsauf, *Poetria Nova*

[Section two]

The Mountain Kiwi

I have very little to say regarding this bird, as I have only seen two of them, and being pushed with hunger, I ate the pair of them, under the circumstances I would have eaten the last of the Dodos.

It is all very well for science, lifting up its hands in horror, at what I once heard called gluttony, but let science tramp through the Westland bush or swamps, for two or three days without food, and find out what hunger is. Besides at the time, which was many years ago, I was not aware that it was an almost extinct bird. Had I known so, I would at least have skinned it and kept the head and feet.

Mr Explorer Douglas, *Birds of South Westland*

[Section three]

There is a theory that when a planet, like our earth, for example, has manifested every form of life, when it has fulfilled itself to the point of exhaustion, it crumbles to bits and is dispersed like star dust throughout the universe. It does not roll on like a dead moon, but explodes, and in the space of a few minutes there is not a trace of it visible in the heavens. In marine life we have a similar effect. It is called implosion. When an amphibian accustomed to the black depths rises above a certain level, when the pressure to which it adapts itself is lifted, the body blows apart, implodes in a million directions. Are we not familiar with this spectacle in the human being also? The Norsemen who went berserk, the Malay who runs amok – are these not examples of implosion and explosion? When the cup is full it runs over. But when the cup and that which it contains are one substance, what then?

Henry Miller, *Sexus*

Good Looks was published in 1982 by Dennis McEldowney at Auckland University Press, and designed by Neysa Moss. It was in five sections, section one beginning with 'The Breakfast Session', two with 'The Swallow', three with 'Loss of the Forest', four with 'Red Horse', while the whole of section five was made up of one poem, 'An Outline'. 'Wingatui' and 'Dettifoss' were placed together under the larger title, 'Two Landscapes'. 'The Anglo-Saxon Onion', 'Riddle', 'Wen', and 'Wulf' are versions of Old English poems. The creature speaking in 'Riddle' is probably an ox.

Zoetropes: Poems 1972–82 was a volume of selected poems published by Bridget Williams at Allen & Unwin/Port Nicholson Press in 1984. The book was designed by Margaret Cochran, and the cover designed by Lindsay Missen, adapting a motif from a nineteenth-century zoetrope strip: a little man whose head happily detached and reattached itself. The poems reprinted here appeared as a group of 'New Poems' in the 1984 *Zoetropes*. All except 'She Says' and 'Breakfast' had previously appeared in *Zoetropes*, published by Chris Elder's Murihiku Press in London in 1981.

Milky Way Bar appeared from Victoria University Press and Carcanet in 1991, with a cover photograph by Peter Black. It was in four sections, section one beginning with 'Out West', section two with 'Miscarriage', section three with 'Synopsis (Handel's *Imeneo*)', while section four comprised the three longer poems, 'Hirohito', 'Brazil', and 'Phar Lap'.

My Sunshine was published in 1996 by Victoria University Press. The cover design was by Fergus Barrowman, while the book's epigraph came from Laurence Sterne's *Tristram Shandy*:

> Digressions, incontestably, are the sunshine; – they are the life, the soul of reading; take them out of this book for instance, – you might as well take the book along with them.

'Hoosh', which in *Collected Poems* appears among the *Antarctic Field Notes*, was originally placed between 'The Adventures of Hillary' and 'Some Screens'.

What to Call Your Child (Auckland: Godwit, 1999) was designed by Sarah Maxey and is the publication which resulted from my term as the inaugural Te Mata Estate Poet Laureate. The book's epigraph, which must be attributed to Marge Simpson, was 'Out of my way, Nature!'. 'Luck: a Villanelle' came into being as a prize ('a love poem by the Poet Laureate') offered at a charity auction to raise money for Alan Duff's 'Books in Homes' scheme; Peter Dunkerley bid $2,500 for the poem, then yet to be written. 'Inesilla', 'Grapes' and 'The Album' are versions of poems by Alexander Pushkin (1799–1837) commissioned by the Folio Society to mark the 200th anni-versary of the poet's birth. 'Colin' was written as one of several collaborative poems with Jenny Bornholdt, Dinah Hawken and Gregory O'Brien using the computing facilities of Victoria Uni-versity's Decision Support Centre. (The process is described in *Landfall* 197, Autumn 1999.) The Antarctic poems from *What to Call Your Child* are now collected under *Antarctic Field Notes*, which has prompted me to add a few contemporaneous outtakes – 'Between Drinks', 'The Gong', 'Fist Round a Magnet', 'Nevertheless' – from *Black Sheep and Other Poems* (Wellington, 2001), a small limited-edition chapbook published and handprinted by Brendan O'Brien.

Antarctic Field Notes: I have brought my Antarctic poems together under this loose title – loose, because 'Hoosh', which first appeared from Anxious Husky Press in 1995 and was then collected in *My Sunshine*, approaches Antarctica through the received frames of science, heroic exploration, and polar tourism, whereas the other poems spring from the firsthand experience of having been there (I travelled as a member of Antarctica New Zealand's Artists to Antarctica programme). Four of the poems – 'The Polar Explorer's Love Song', 'Deep Field Song', 'Antarctic Stone' and 'Visiting Mr Shackleton' – first appeared in *Homelight*, a limited-edition miscellany by Chris Orsman, Nigel Brown and Bill Manhire, which was entirely written and published in Antarctica in January 1998.

'The Next Thousand' was commissioned by Anthony Hubbard for the *Sunday Star-Times*'s millennium supplement *2000 AD* (Auckland, January 2000).

Only when you assemble a book of this sort do you realise how much *character* the individual volumes from which it is made actually possess. My thanks to all the publishers, designers and – in the case of *Picnic* – handsetters who contributed to the original books. My thanks to Greg O'Brien for the wonderfully equestrian cover of this book (though I feel bound to say that I have never ridden a horse in my life). And, though this goes without saying, my particular thanks to Fergus Barrowman at Victoria University Press and Michael Schmidt at Carcanet. I am glad that they have stuck by me over the years.

Acknowledgements are also made to the editors of the following publications, where many of the poems first appeared: *Affairs, An Anthology of Twentieth Century New Zealand Poetry, Between These Hills, Causley at 70, Cave, The Caxton Press Anthology: New Zealand Poetry 1972-86, Dem Dichter des Lesens: Gedichte für Paul Hoffman, Homelight, Edge, etymspheres, The Ear in a Wheatfield, Grand Piano, The Inward Sun, Island Magazine, Islands, Kunapipi, Landfall, London Magazine, London Review of Books, Meanjin, Metro, Morepork, The New Criterion, New Poetry, New Zealand Books, New Zealand Herald, NZ Listener, NZU Arts Festival Yearbook, Numbers, Of Pavlova, Poetry and Paradigms, The Penguin Book of Contemporary New Zealand Poetry, PN Review, Poems for Charles Causley, Poems for the Eighties, Poetry Australia, Poetry New Zealand, The Present Tense, Printout, Quote Unquote, Rambling Jack, Review, Spleen, Sport, Stand, Strawberry Fields, Sunday Star-Times, Ten Modern New Zealand Poets, Timber, Tussock & Rushing Rivers, Times Literary Supplement, Verse, The Young New Zealand Poets.*

BM
Wellington, March 2001

INDEX OF TITLES

INDEX OF FIRST LINES